THE STARTUP LEGAL GUIDE

The Disaster-Free Startup and Fundraising Handbook for Founders and Investors

JERRY KU AND HAN XU

THE STARTUP LEGAL GUIDE
The Disaster-Free Startup and Fundraising Handbook for Founders and Investors by Jerry Ku and Han Xu

Aktive Group Pte. Ltd. 10 Anson Road #10-11 International Plaza Singapore 079903

E-mail: publisher@aktive.com.sg
Website: http://www.aktive.com.sg

ISBN (Paperback): 978-981-14-4557-6

National Library Board, Singapore Cataloguing-in-Publication Data

Name(s): Ku, Jerry. | Han, Xu, author. Title: The startup legal guide : the disaster-free startup and fundraising handbook for founders and investors / Jerry Ku, Han Xu. Description: Singapore : Aktive Group Pte. Ltd., [2020] Identifier(s): OCN 1131709187 | ISBN 978-981-14-4557-6 (paperback) Subject(s): LCSH: New business enterprises--Management. | New business enterprises--Planning. | Entrepreneurship. Classification: DDC 658.11--dc23

Disclaimer

The materials presented in this book are for informational and educational purposes only. While care has been taken to ensure accuracy and timeliness, the publisher and the authors make no expressed or implied warranty of any kind and assume no responsibility for errors or omissions. Nothing contained in this book shall be construed as providing legal advice. Readers shall engage their own counsel in handling any specific case. No liability is assumed for incidental or consequential damages in connection with or arising out of the use of the information contained within.

Jerry: To my companions on these voyages

Xu: To my most amazing family

Contents

Introduction

Creating a startup company is like giving birth to a baby. This is not just a figure of speech – when a company is formed, the law treats it as a separate legal person with real rights and obligations of its own.

What do we usually do before we have a baby? We buy tons of books on pregnancy and parenting, ask friends and experts for tips and advice, spend hours online doing extensive research on the birth process, breastfeeding, baby food, how many hours of sleep babies need, what to do when they are sick, how to babyproof our house to prevent injuries, etc..

On the other hand, while most entrepreneur "parents" have high hopes for their baby company to grow at superspeed and become Hercules after just a few years, most of them don't bother to spend any time finding out how to raise strong and healthy children, or how to navigate their babies through the minefield called "fundraising".

In our voyage as startup lawyers, we've supported both the success and the struggles of many startup companies and the entrepreneurs behind them. We repeatedly noticed the importance of knowing and doing the "right" thing from the very beginning. Just like children, in order to be competitive and successful, a company needs to form good habits, build up a healthy body, have the right education and avoid doing stupid things that get them into trouble.

This book is written with the intention to explain all the key issues a startup company is likely to encounter and to point out the location of the common pitfalls. It also sets out market convention and trends in the startup industry as a reference point for founders and investors.

Entrepreneurs can read this book as a "parenting" guide, with practical "parenting" tips illustrated and summarized in one place. Investors can also benefit from this book. With the anatomy of the company and the funding process explained in great detail, investors can carry out due diligence much more effectively and have a better understanding of key funding terms.

During the process of writing this book, we have tried to illustrate complicated issues with specific examples and avoided legalese whenever possible. While the main text sets out the basic information, we expanded the topic slightly in the footnotes. For readers who already have basic knowledge on the topic, you will gain more insights from the footnotes.

The startup life is a difficult path, one filled with extreme challenges and rewards. With this book, we hope to shed some light on this demanding journey and make the life of entrepreneurs and investors a little easier.

May you realize your dream and find your pot of gold! Bon voyage!

Jerry Ku and Han Xu

Chapter 1
Company Formation

In this chapter, we will cover some fundamentals of forming a startup company. While this chapter is geared towards entrepreneurs, it is written from the perspective of preparing the company so that it is suitable and ready for external funding. Thus, investors will also benefit by being aware of key questions to ask during early discussions with potential portfolio companies prior to legal advisors getting involved.

Formation

As an entrepreneur, once you have an idea that you would like to pursue, typically the next logical step is to form a legal entity, so that liabilities from the business pursuit is separate from you as an individual and does not become your personal liability. Having the startup in a separate legal entity also facilitates external funding. After all, you would have a hard time dividing yourself up into parcels of economic interests, whereas a legal entity can easily issue stock and other instruments evidencing, or conveying the right to acquire, legal ownership.

Incorporator

While the first order of business on the legal front is setting up a company, "setting up the company" in different jurisdictions means different things. For example, if the company is being set up in the Cayman Islands, typically that means retaining an agent to compile the paperwork and submit them with the Cayman Islands government. After submission, the agent will continue to handle routine corporate matters for the company, including updating the various registers of directors, officers and members.

In contrast, if the company is being set up in the State of Delaware (of the United States), an agent would still handle the initial submission with the Delaware government, but the paperwork would be in the name of an individual who serves as the company's *incorporator,* who may be someone at the company or with the agent.[1] For a Delaware company, after the submission of paperwork, corporate actions become a very private matter that are handled internally by the *secretary* of the company.[2]

---

1   For the purposes of this book, we will focus primarily on the Cayman Islands and Delaware because of their prevalence as jurisdictions of choice for venture-backed startup companies and because other popular jurisdictions such as the British Virgin Islands and California will have corporate codes that bear strong resemblance to either the Cayman Islands or Delaware. We have also included information on Singapore as this book is geared towards startups in Asia.

2   A mistake made by many Delaware companies is leaving the incorporator in place. As we will describe below, the proper sequence of incorporation entails the incorporator adopting the bylaws, appointing the initial directors and then resigning as the incorporator. Failure to do so promptly incurs the risk of the company being unable to complete its corporate formalities

Comparatively, to set up a Singapore company, Singaporeans and Singapore permanent residents can directly apply online through the website of the Accounting and Corporate Regulatory Authority of Singapore (www.acra.gov.sg). Foreigners need to retain a registered filing agent (e.g., law firm, accounting firm or corporate secretarial firm) to submit the online application on his or her behalf. There is no concept of a separate "incorporator".

Directors and officers

In both the Cayman Islands and Delaware, the company is formed once the agent or the incorporator has signed and submitted the formation documents.[3] Next, either the agent or the incorporator will need to appoint the initial directors of the company. In Singapore, the formation process is completed once the online approval for incorporation is received from the Accounting and Corporate Regulatory Authority of Singapore. The list of director(s) needs to be submitted in advance in the application of incorporation.

Under the corporate laws of a vast majority of jurisdictions, the *board of directors* is the ultimate decision-making body with respect to the operations of a company. This is a key concept that

---

because it cannot locate the incorporator at a later date to sign the necessary documents. The incorporator should also heed the benefit of resigning promptly because, prior to the appointment of directors and resignation, the incorporator is the de facto legal representative of the company and potentially liable for its actions.

3   With respect to Delaware companies, internal corporate matters such as board composition and manner of election, officers and powers and shareholder meetings and notice mechanics are typically embodied in a private instrument called the bylaws, unlike a Cayman company, for which such provisions would be contained in the memorandum and articles of association filed with the government. The bylaws are typically adopted by the incorporator and subsequently ratified by the initial directors.

we will see repeatedly when we get into financing terms.[4] In most jurisdictions, such as Cayman, Delaware and Singapore, directors may be but do not have to be shareholders of the company. In certain South East Asia jurisdictions such as the Philippines, the directors are required to hold nominal amounts of shares in the company.

With the initial directors in place, they typically will do several things. Most importantly, they will (1) appoint *officers* – the company's president, chief executive officer, treasurer (or chief financial officer) and secretary, (2) approve opening one or more bank accounts (typically banks will want to see board resolutions for approving bank account opening as one of the account opening documents)[5] and (3) approve the initial share issuances to whomever the initial shareholders may be (typically, the entrepreneur/founding team).

Share issuance

At this point, the company essentially has no value because it is a newly incorporated entity. Typically, the issuance price for shares to the entrepreneur can be made at nominal value (e.g., par value). An entrepreneur may elect to pay the purchase price

---

4   In some jurisdictions, there is a separate governing body called the *board of supervisors* whose duty is to, as the name suggests, supervise the board of director's exercise of powers. Since jurisdictions with such setup is in the minority when it comes to venture-backed startup companies in the authors' experience, we will merely note here that such possibility exists.

5   Apart from practical necessities for having the company's own bank account, from a corporate law perspective, a company maintaining its own separate bank account, with funds and expenditures clearly distinct and separate from the entrepreneurs' personal funds, is one of the key elements for corporations being able to maintain its limited liability status vis-à-vis third parties.

with cash or by contributing all intellectual properties pertaining to the company. The latter has the advantage of combining (1) payment for shares and (2) contribution of intellectual properties to the company (which, as we will cover below, is a necessary step in the incorporation of an entity ready for external funding) in one step. It is also a good fact against any future challenge by the tax authority that the price for the shares was too cheap (especially if the company experiences explosive growth), since the exchange of intellectual properties for share issuance (of a newly established shell with no value) must logically be an even exchange.

Where exchanging shares for intellectual properties may not be the best arrangement includes situations where the entrepreneur has no intellectual properties other than a business plan to contribute (which the U.S. tax authorities may argue means the entrepreneur has not given anything of value to the company and instead received the shares for services or anticipated services to the company[6]), and/or the entrepreneur is still working at a different company that potentially has claims on the intellectual properties, particularly if such company is in the same or similar field. In those situations, paying for the shares with cash may be the entrepreneur's best option.

---

6   Being deemed to have received equity in exchange for services typically results in the entrepreneur being deemed to have received income in the form of stock. This would be a very undesirable situation because tax payments due will need to be paid in cash, but the stock that has been deemed an income is illiquid. Entrepreneurs would do well to consult with accountants and lawyers in advance of share issuance to avoid such pitfall.

Example:

> Let's introduce the "protagonist" of the book: ABC Company. We will repeatedly come back to ABC Company to flesh out the concepts we cover in this book. For now, let's keep things simple and assume that you and 2 co-founders formed ABC Company, and 1 million shares of capital stock is issued to each co-founder (i.e., a total of 3 million shares of capital stock issued initially).

Founder Share Vesting

With respect to a company with multiple members on the founding team, it is advisable to at least consider implementing vesting restrictions on the shares issued to the founders, whereby full unencumbered ownership of the shares "vest" over time, with any "unvested" shares being subject to some type of forfeiture.[7] The reason for that is mainly because a startup is not a fully formed business – it takes a lot of time, energy and funding to grow

---

7   Outright forfeiture is somewhat rare; more typical conventions include repurchase by the company "at cost", a refund of the founder's purchase money in return for the unvested shares) or nominal consideration (i.e., company being entitled to repurchase the unvested shares for $1.00 in total). Note if the relevant company is incorporated in jurisdictions with restrictions on reduction of capital (such as China), forfeiture and repurchase are typically not an option because they may be viewed as a reduction of capital, so the workaround is the redistribution of unvested shares to the remaining founding team. For jurisdictions with limited restrictions on reduction of capital (such as Hong Kong and Singapore), repurchase of shares can be done by the company only if certain statutory requirements (e.g., solvency statement etc.) are met. It is recommended to draft in the flexibility to facilitate both the capital reduction by the company or the redistribution of the shares to other entities in the documents setting out the vesting terms.

the startup into a viable business. In that sense, shares issued to founders consist of primarily forward-looking component, i.e., the value that a founder will contribute towards making the company a success. Therefore, to the extent things happen and circumstances change, and a founder has to leave the company, voluntarily or involuntarily, it is typically viewed as grossly unfair if such founder will no longer contribute to building the company yet will continue to enjoy the fruits of the remaining founders' labor through appreciation in value of all the stock in the company he or she was initially issued. In addition, the role and function of such departed founder will likely need to be filled by one or more new hires, who will typically expect an equity component to their compensation, and the shares repurchased from the departed founder can be "recycled" to make new equity grants to the replacement hire.

Market convention for vesting is that shares vest over 4 years in equal monthly, quarterly or annual installments. Some co-founders may also agree to a "4 years vesting with a 1 year cliff" arrangement, which means ¼ of the shares will vest at the end of the 1 year period, the rest vest over the remaining 3 years in equal monthly, quarterly or annual installments. The vesting start date may be pegged to the date the company is formed, the date the shares are issued or when a founder started working on the project, to give credit to the founder time already spent working towards the company's success.[8]

---

8   Alternatively, vesting restrictions can be placed on less than 100% of the shares, with the unrestricted portion representing "credit" to the founder. The two approaches are not entirely fungible, though. For example, a founder can receive credit for a year already spent working on the project with an earlier vesting start date, which means vesting started a year prior (which means 25% is already vested), and the founder only has 3 more years to fully vest in the remaining 75%. Contrast that with the alternative arrangement,

Lastly, the founders can agree on certain triggers that will accelerate the rate of vesting to provide for unexpected successes and unforeseen tragedies. A good legal advisor will advise on arrangements that are market convention and defensible at the time of a venture capital investment. Investors similarly have a strong desire to make sure founders are properly incentivized to remain with the company and work towards its success, so they will pay close attention to vesting arrangements. Deviating too far from the market norm is tantamount to an invitation to renegotiate the whole scheme.

We will revisit the concept of vesting later, as this topic will come up in the context of employee stock ownership programs as well.

Example:

> You decided to place a 4-year, monthly vesting restriction on ABC Company's founder shares, so for each co-founder's 1 million shares (including yourself), the shares will become vested at the rate of 20833.333 shares per month over 48 months. You also decided to put in an acceleration term where if ABC Company is sold and a founder is terminated thereafter without cause, then all remaining unvested shares become immediately vested (this is typically referred to as "double trigger" acceleration).
>
> Three weeks after you and your co-founders (who are also your "best friends forever", or "BFFs") form ABC Company, one of your co-founder's wife decides that he needs to get a "real job" and that co-founder has to leave (true story*), ABC Company will be able to repurchase all 1 million shares held by that co-founder because none of it has vested. The shares

---

which is to subject only 75% of the shares to vesting, with the other 25% being unrestricted outright. In such arrangement, the founder still must work the full 4 years to fully vest in the remaining 75%.

repurchased are canceled, and the 2 million shares that you and the remaining co-founder hold now represent 100% ownership of ABC Company.

*   This example deviates from the true story on which it is based in that the BFFs in the real life example did not put any vesting restrictions on their shares since they were BFFs. Fortunately, as between keeping 100% of the shares or remaining BFFs, the departing co-founder chose the latter, so there was still a happy ending to the story.

Right of first refusal

Even after shares are fully vested, they would typically be subject to a right of first refusal by the company against any proposed transfers. The reason this term makes sense (and should be applied to all issuances out of the ESOP (discussed in the next chapter) as well[9])) is because this term gives companies the ability to prevent their shares from ending up in the hands of undesirable buyers (for example, a competitor). A right of first refusal restriction does have a chilling effect on the transferability of the company's shares because potential buyers are less inclined to spend the time and resources structuring and negotiating a share purchase if the company has the right to match the terms and acquire the shares.[10]

---

9   However, unlike the lock-up provision discussed immediately below, investors are much less likely to accept this transfer restriction impeding their ability to sell or transfer their shares.

10 But one can also argue a right of first refusal obligation has the effect of forcing potential buyers to overpay for shares to prevent or discourage the company from exercising its right.

Lock-up

Underwriters who are responsible for selling the company's securities in an IPO will invariably demand that the company's shareholders execute a lock-up agreement that obligates them not to sell or otherwise dispose any company securities during a lock-up period (typically 180 days) following an IPO. Without a lock-up, shareholders would be free to sell their shares, which in turn would create a glut of the company's shares in the market and depress share price. Lock-up agreements are essentially universally required by underwriters, but individual shareholders are far less likely to sign a lock-up agreement when they know an IPO is imminent, so the company needs to make it a standard practice to include lock-up provisions in all securities issuance documents upfront. This is true for any issuances pursuant to the ESOP as well as issuances to investors.

Meetings, quorum for meetings and written actions, and minute books

Once the proper corporate formalities are in place – the company formed by the incorporator or agent, action having been taken by the incorporator or agent to appoint the initial directors, the initial directors having ratified the charter documents and appointed the initial officers and approved initial share issuances to the founders – all of the documents that have been signed to implement the foregoing should be filed in the company's *minute books*. The minute books, as the name suggests, contains all the minutes of meetings of the board of directors and meetings of shareholders, as well as other actions taken, and resolutions adopted in writing without a meeting. The minute books will also frequently contain other important corporate records such as the shareholder ledger/register of shareholders, copies of share certificates, share issuance instruments and related documents, etc.. The minute books are typically kept at the company's offices or with the company's law firm. Well-maintained minute books are desirable from a corporate governance perspective, and review of minute books is invariably a key task for any legal due diligence of a company.

Holding regular board meetings is generally viewed as good corporate governance because such meetings provide a forum for vigorous discussion and deliberation of important corporate matters among the directors. The formality and on-the-record nature of the occasion is generally thought to encourage participants to be more mindful of their duties to the company as directors, as opposed to, for example, a telephone call between two co-founders who are directors as well as shareholders, who may not be as diligent about distinguishing their various roles and perspectives.

Also, it is important to hold regular board meetings and keep good minutes of the proceedings because in a vast majority of jurisdictions, there is the concept of *piercing the corporate veil*, which means that if a company is run as if it is essentially the entrepreneur's alter ego, then in the event of a claim against the company, whether arising out of debt or other liabilities, the limited liability status of the corporate entity will be disregarded, and the company's claimant or debtor can bring an action directly against the entrepreneur and other shareholders of the company. Two classic evidences for a company merely being an alter ego of the entrepreneur are (1) commingling of the entrepreneurs' personal funds with the company's corporate funds and (2) the lack of corporate formalities such as holding regular board meetings to discuss corporate matters.

Lastly, another reason why maintaining good minute books is important for companies planning to obtain external funding is because minute books are central to an investor's legal due diligence of the company. In that respect, a company's corporate records, as embodied in its minute books, demonstrate good corporate governance and allow an investor to piece together the corporation actions taken up to that point. Therefore, in addition to the actions taken in connection with incorporation, to the extent the company has adopted a share plan, granted options or issued additional shares to new founding team members, it is essential that such actions are all adopted pursuant to the requisite corporate formalities and are well-documented in board meeting minutes (and any requisite shareholder meeting minutes) and are filed in the company's minute books. This is so that the company has a record of such actions having been taken, and so that the records ready for examination when an investor conducts legal due diligence on the company.

Indemnification

As we have explained, shareholders' liability for the acts and liabilities of the company is limited. However, the same cannot be said for directors of the company, who are liable to the company's shareholders, the company's employees, as well as to outside parties under certain circumstances. Because of this, it is a good idea to enter into an indemnification agreement with each director (and investors typically require the company to do so with its director designees).[11] The purpose of the indemnification agreement is primarily twofold: (1) for the company to indemnify the director against liabilities, subject to certain exceptions and (2)

---

11   Corporate law of most jurisdictions favored by venture investors as well as most standard company charter documents provide for indemnification, but it is market practice for companies to have an indemnification agreement with directors so there is direct contractual privity with respect to this obligation.

for the company to commit to advancing payment for expenses incurred by a director, so the director will not be out-of-pocket for too long defending against claims.

Note that because directors are inherently an interested party in indemnification agreements, typically shareholder approval is solicited for the form of such agreements.

Government permits and licenses

Once the internal corporate formalities of the company are in place, it is then time to obtain the necessary permits and licenses for the company to conduct its proposed business.[12] As one might expect, different jurisdictions will have different licensing and permitting requirements. For example, in the United States and Singapore, a company is deemed to be properly formed and ready for business when the incorporating documents are filed and accepted, so a company can be up and running in as little as one day and start hiring employees and entering into contracts. In contrast, in China, the incorporation process typically requires several weeks and is not deemed complete until approvals and permits from several departments have been obtained. In addition, as an example, to conduct business over the internet in China, an Internet Content Provider license is required. Because different jurisdictions have different requirements, it is a good idea to consult with experienced professionals on the permits and licenses required for the company's proposed business.

---

12 As we will discuss below, if the company itself is set up in a jurisdiction that is different from where it will be conducting its business (which is typically the case for a company set up in the Cayman Islands), it will almost always need to set up a subsidiary in the jurisdiction where it will be conducting its business (other than companies set up in one U.S. state and primarily operates in another U.S. state).

Founders and other service providers

Employment and consulting agreements

This may come as a surprise to some, but each member of the company's initial founding team needs to sign an offer letter or employment agreement with the company. The reason for that is twofold. First, many jurisdictions have various rules governing employment arrangements that cannot be opted out (even by founders of a company) and therefore should be formalized in a written document to avoid future disputes, either between the company on the one hand and a founding team member on the other hand, or between the company and/or founding team member on the one hand and the government on the other hand.[13] Second, the offer letter or employment agreement will also form the basis for the company's ownership of any intellectual properties created by the founding team members.[14] We will go into more detail later on the assignment of intellectual properties by service providers to the company.

A word of caution before signing up services providers

---

13 For example, minimum wage and overtime rules are inflexible in many jurisdictions, so it would be best to formalize employment terms in a written instrument instead of defaulting to applicable statutory terms that are typically unfavorable to the company. Another labor relations matter that governments are keenly interested in is tax withholding, which is also best set forth in written form instead of letting default statutory provisions that are typically government-favorable to govern.

14 It is also essential that, to the extent the founding team members have not contributed their existing intellectual properties in exchange for shares in the company, they should enter into a technology assignment agreement covering all pre-employment intellectual properties so there is no ambiguity as to ownership of the intellectual properties that the company needs to conduct its business.

directly with the main company not located in the country where the service will be provided: many countries are deeply skeptical (to put it mildly) of offshore corporations, especially ones incorporated in tax-free jurisdictions (such as the Cayman Islands), and a myriad of tax laws have been enacted to set up a dragnet to catch such corporations and ensure they pay local taxes. To avoid being caught up in such laws, it is typically recommended that a company form separate subsidiaries for each jurisdiction in which it has substantive presence, with hiring and contracting being done by the subsidiary instead of the offshore parent company.

For example, if a Cayman Islands company is employing people in Singapore, it should set up a Singapore subsidiary so that Singapore-related revenues and expenses are compartmentalized in the Singapore subsidiary, and Singapore government will have less nexus to come after the Cayman Islands parent company for taxes on the income generated from operating in other countries.[15] For local operations in their infancy, sometimes companies can get away with hiring one or two local service providers and put them on consulting arrangements. Doing so is a stopgap measure, entails varying degrees of risk depending on the jurisdiction involved and other facts and circumstances and should only be used sparingly.[16]

---

15 Keep in mind that such structure generates intra-group services, income and expense and related transfer pricing issues that are beyond the scope of this book; a company should consult its tax/accounting advisors.

16 Countries have a strong interest in invalidating such arrangements from both the perspective of employee protection (i.e., protecting its citizenry from foreign exploitation) as well as from a revenue perspective (employment relationships typically generate tax withholdings and social insurance contributions by the employer, which is typically not the case when it comes to consulting relationships).

Confidentiality and inventions assignment

Another key item in ensuring the robustness of a company's formation, and one that we have repeatedly touched on, is the company's ownership of intellectual properties developed by its service providers (including the founding team). In some jurisdictions, especially ones with systemically poor protection of intellectual properties, this task is frequently overlooked or assigned less importance. However, among the various barrier to entry (funding, market share, technology), intellectual property is arguably the one that is least dependent on facts and circumstances beyond a company's control. And because legal barriers to entry represent a competitive advantage, protection of intellectual properties creates intrinsic value for the company.

Therefore, venture-backed startup companies will typically require its service providers to execute what is known as a *confidential information and inventions assignment agreement* (which some also refer to as *proprietary information and inventions agreement* or by some other name) with all its service providers. This agreement is comprised of three key components. The first is a confidentiality obligation owed by the service providers to the company, which means service providers have to keep any company information they come into contact with confidential so that the company's information does not become known by others.[17]

The second key component to such an agreement is that the service provider agrees to assign to the Company the rights and title to all intellectual properties developed by him or her in the

---

17 In addition, the company may have confidential information of third parties and owe a duty to keep such information confidential, and without a confidentiality obligation from its service providers, the company would have no means of discharging its obligations to such third parties. Please refer to chapter 7 for an overview of the confidential information and inventions assignment agreement.

course of working for the company.[18] The company has every interest to make sure that the fruit of such labor is owned by the company and not by the service provider, and the authors' view is not to leave such critical company interests to the labor codes of local jurisdictions that may or may not fully vest title of intellectual properties in the employers in the absence of a written contract.

The third key component, and one that is often overlooked even by practitioners, is a perpetual, royalty-free, sublicensable, worldwide license to use the intellectual rights belonging to the service provider that the service provider used or incorporated into the company's products or services. This prevents a company's service providers from maliciously or unwittingly embedding his or her intellectual property into the company's products and services and later try to claim title, ownership or right to receive royalties from the company.[19]

Moonlighting

The discussion above provides a good segue into a related topic, which is the topic of moonlighting. At the infancy of a company, a lot of service providers (particularly the founding team) typically have a day job because the company doesn't have the money to pay salaries. Such service providers would then have to

---

18 The exact breadth of this assignment differs by jurisdiction. For example, some jurisdictions permit the scope of such forcible assignment to cover anything having to do with the business of the company, even if developed within a certain time period after the service provider leaves the company's employment.

19 This goes beyond a simple quitclaim of title or non-assertion agreement because the company's customers and investors also have a strong interest in ensuring the integrity of the company's intellectual property ownership, and quitclaim, non-assertion and other arrangement that simply amounts to an agreement of *no contest* is generally viewed as insufficient.

start as consultants for the company while keeping a full-time job that pays the bills. This is understandable but is also a very risky proposition for the company because this arrangement creates ambiguity in the ownership of intellectual properties created by such service providers.

Recall that a company should have a contract with its service providers to assign to the company ownership of all intellectual properties developed by such service providers. However, the other companies that such service providers are working at will very likely similarly have an intellectual property assignment/ownership arrangement in place. So the question then becomes: when did these service providers develop the intellectual properties in question, for whom, on whose time, and using whose resources, as these are all factors that go into ascertaining ownership.[20] This is an especially thorny issue if the companies with competing ownership claims are operating in the same industry or adjacent industries. This is also an issue with respect to service providers who are affiliated with governments and academic institutions, because those entities also have an interest in making sure that all intellectual properties developed by their service providers are owned by such institutions.

These pitfalls are especially important to keep in mind as you think about establishing a company, developing its intellectual properties and staffing the initial team, because your potential investors will certainly take a deep dive during business and legal due diligence to ensure the process was copacetic. It is also crucial for investors to remember to ask entrepreneurs where they were working and what were they doing prior to and at the time

---

20 And claim may be established from something as innocuous as using the company's email account, sending results from the university's computer lab or asking a doctoral student to help out with some experiments.

they were setting up their company.[21]

Intellectual property

Confidentiality and NDA

Protection of intellectual property does not end with the company's service providers signing up to the various obligations discussed above. It also entails vigilance vis-à-vis third parties. It is therefore critical that before the company discloses its information to third parties, the recipient is first required to sign a confidentiality or nondisclosure agreement.[22] As one might expect, such agreement should, at a minimum, contain an obligation by the receiving party to hold the information confidential and not disclose it to anyone else.

Such agreements typically also include: (1) an obligation not to use disclosed information outside of a very narrow scope of permitted uses (e.g., evaluating the company's technology), (2) an undertaking that information should be returned or destroyed upon the disclosing party's request and (3) disclaimers by the disclosing party that no license is granted, and no warranties are given by virtue of the disclosure.[23]

---

21 Instead of recounting the parade of horribles, interested readers can look up the dispute between Mattel Inc. and MGA Entertainment Inc. over the Bratz line of dolls.

22 Note that the vast majority of investors will not agree to signing confidentiality/nondisclosure agreements, because they generally receive many pitches containing similar ideas and concepts, and they cannot afford to make investment in one or a few of them and risk being accused by the rest of having breached confidentiality obligations.

23 If you are an entrepreneur, and the receiving party wants to negotiate permitted disclosures or uses, including a so-called "residuals clause", that would be the time to pick the telephone and call your legal counsel (if you had not done so already).

Registrations

The other aspect of developing a robust intellectual property portfolio entails registering for protection with the government, whether in the form of trademark protection, patent protection or, less frequently, copyright protection. This is also a topic that a startup company needs to think about (and that investors typically place a lot of value in) because these registrations also represent barriers to entry. Different jurisdictions have different requirements with respect to priority and disqualifying circumstances that are beyond the scope of this book, but a general rule of thumb is that time (and with respect to patents, secrecy) is of the essence for applications.

Contracts

It never ceases to amaze us how many companies do a terrible job at the simple task of keeping a good file on signed contracts. Just like the minute books, a good contracts file is essential for accurate record keeping (both from a legal perspective and from a financials perspective, as discussed below), and ensures a smooth process during business, financial and legal due diligence review of the company by outside parties (including by prospective investors).

Startup companies should be diligent about keeping clean and clear copies of fully signed agreements, amendments and ancillary documents (including ones signed with employees, but those would likely go into a separate human resources file instead of into the contracts file).[24] This permits companies to

---

24 Depending on a company's industry, sometimes the prevailing practice is doing business via purchase orders and invoices, but care must be taken to make sure that purchase orders and invoices do not reference other documents, terms or conditions that the company has not seen. Also, in the absence of specific terms and conditions,

keep track of, and for prospective investors to quickly understand, the company's rights and obligations with respect to third parties.

Financial statements

On the topic of contracts as they relate to financial statements, the numbers in the ledgers, whether they are in the form of simple management accounts or in full-blown financial statements, should be supported by and consistent with signed contracts. Conversely, well-prepared management accounts and financial statements will offer a very good roadmap for prospective investors to conduct due diligence on a company's material contracts and obligations.

Litigation

For companies, it is a good idea to keep good records of written correspondences from third parties involving potential disputes, even benign-looking "invitations" to discuss license arrangements. In subsequent chapters, it will become apparent why this is important for companies. Apart from risk management and good corporate hygiene, prospective investors will also conduct due diligence on these materials to assess potential risks and determine whether some combination of pricing and legal structuring is warranted to address these risks (or in extreme cases, abandon the investment altogether).

---

a company relying on purchase orders and invoices to do business should also understand the implied warranties and obligations it is signing up to under local laws in connection with delivering its products and services in the absence of written terms. For this reason, most companies would rather have a detailed agreement (or perhaps a master agreement) setting forth such details rather than leaving it to local law or, worse, whims of local judge or jury.

Chapter 2
Employee Stock Ownership Plan

An important component of most startup companies is an employee stock ownership program, commonly referred to as *ESOP*. An ESOP is particularly important in the context of a startup company because the value of a startup company is typically expected to grow very quickly, so when people decide to work for startup companies, they join with the dream of working for the next Google or Facebook and be financially rewarded from the increase in value of the equity compensation they receive.

However, equity compensation is not a free lunch for startup companies or their employees, because it represents dilution of the founding team's stake in the company as well as the employee sacrificing some cash compensation. As a rule, the younger a startup company is, the more generous it will be with equity compensation because (1) younger companies have less available cash to offer market rate cash compensation, (2) earlier hires tend to be more crucial to a startup company and (3) the value of each unit of equity is lower when a company is younger.

Outside of the purely economic perspective, another useful purpose of ESOP is to identify prospective hires who have true alignment and passion for the startup company's vision, demonstrated by the willingness to forgo immediate cash benefits in order to work at the startup company towards the fruition of a shared vision. Having prospective employees weigh offers between, for example, going to work for Microsoft and getting market rate cash compensation but equity compensation with relatively limited upside and joining a startup company at below market rate cash compensation but with equity compensation that has a huge upside, helps a startup company recruit more suitable hires just by virtue of filtering out candidates whose career and financial objectives are not aligned with what the startup company has to offer.

In making that decision, a startup company's employees are also, consciously or unconsciously, making an investment decision in the company. This is extremely powerful both from a motivational perspective and because such investment opportunities are simply not available to the general public. For example, the only way to get your hands on Google stock back in 1997 was either being a venture capitalist or going to work for Google.

In addition, equity awards promote retention at the company because, as we will further discuss below, full ownership of the award is typically settled over time and tied to continuous services at the company (i.e., the concept of "vesting", which we previously discussed in the context of founder shares), and when a service provider terminates his or her relationship with the company, whether voluntarily or involuntarily, vesting stops, and any unvested or unexercised portion of the award typically reverts back to the company either immediately at the time of the termination or within a relatively short period thereafter (generally 3 months after termination).

While the rationale for equity incentives is largely consistent regardless of the form of the award, different instruments are available to achieve that purpose. The three most commonly used instruments for a private company are options, restricted stock and restricted stock units. We will explain the pros and cons of each instrument in turn.

Example:

> Your ABC Company is hiring. The founders decide to allocate 5% to employees. ABC Company therefore reserves 105,263 shares (2,000,000 founders shares + 105,263 ESOP shares = 2,105,263 total shares; 5% of 2,105,263 shares = 105,263 shares) in its ESOP.

Options

Options should be a familiar instrument to just about anyone who has had any involvement with the startup sector or technology industry. It is popular because it is set up to incentivize employee contributions toward overall growth of the company.

Options are, in a nutshell, simply contractual obligations of the company to deliver its stock in the future at a pre-determined price (typically referred to as the *exercise price* or the *strike price*) when certain conditions are met. The exercise price of options is usually pegged to the fair value of the company at the time an option is granted. Therefore, option awards granted under an ESOP would start to accrue value only when the company's value increases, thereby incentivizing the recipients to work toward that common goal.

In the case of startup companies, the value of the enterprise can (and ideally should) undergo exponential growth from seed funding through each successive equity funding until the company's initial public offering. The wealth creation power of option awards therefore lies in the number of shares covered by an option award as well as the magnitude of the price increase from the exercise price.[25]

The earlier an employee joins a startup company, the more likely this person will receive a greater number of option shares at a lower strike price, giving rise to the phenomena of overnight millionaires for early employees at companies like Google and Facebook when they go public.

Special U.S. tax considerations – 409A

For any companies with prospective option recipients who are U.S. taxpayers, note that U.S. tax rules impose a special excise tax on any options granted with an exercise price below fair market value of the underlying shares at the time of the grant.[26]

---

25 The unhappy situation where an option's exercise price is more than the fair value of the underlying shares is referred to as an *underwater option.*

26 And some U.S. states impose an additional excise tax on top of the U.S. federal excise tax. For example, the total excise tax for a U.S. taxpayer who is also a California resident taxpayer would be an additional 25% tax (20% U.S. federal excise tax; 5% California excise tax) on any gains on the option, which, when combined with the regular U.S. federal and California income taxes on the gains, basically wipe out a majority of the gain on an option.

Since the primary purpose of making equity incentive grants is to incentivize and drive employee behavior towards building a more valuable company, it would be a real shame if the value represented by option instruments is wiped out by taxation. That is why it is imperative that option grants to recipients who are U.S. taxpayers are made with the exercise price set at the fair market value at the time of the grant and not at some arbitrary price point as some companies are wont to do.

To establish fair market value, the most straightforward approach is to obtain an independent third-party appraisal of the fair market value of the company's shares, but that costs money and is only good for 12 months (or a shorter period of time if the company has a significant milestone before the expiration date, such as raising a new round of equity funding). Therefore, whether your company needs to obtain such valuation report (at least initially, when the company is cash-strapped) really depends on the number and importance of the recipients who are U.S. taxpayers.

Singapore Tax Considerations

Different from the U.S. tax rules, Singapore simply tax the "gains" from the option with no additional excise tax even when the option exercise price is below the fair market value at the time of the grant. "Gains" are calculated as:

- (when no selling restriction is imposed on the underlying shares) open market price of the share on the date of exercise less the exercise price; or
- (when selling restriction is imposed on the underlying shares) open market price of the share on the date the selling restriction is lifted less the exercise price.

Tax on options are payable in the year when the option is exercised (if no selling restriction on the shares) or in the year when the selling restriction is lifted (if selling restriction is imposed on the shares). Very often, employees do not have enough cash to meet their tax obligations when the option is exercised as they may not wish to sell their newly acquired shares immediately. In order to ease this cash flow problems of employees, Singapore tax rules[27] allow tax on ESOP to be deferred for up to 5 years (subject to an interest charge) if the set criteria are met.

It is also important for foreign employees working in Singapore to note that a foreign employee is deemed to have obtained taxable gains from unexercised or restricted option when he or she ceases to work in Singapore with the company that granted him or her the option. The final gains from unexercised option or restricted option are deemed to be income derived by the employee one month before the date of cessation of employment or the date the right or benefit is granted, whichever is later. This includes both foreigners and Singapore permanent residents leaving Singapore permanently or posted overseas for work.

As an alternative to the "deemed exercise rule", the employer company can also track and report the "income realization event" to the tax authority to assess, at a later date, the actual gains of a foreign employee who is leaving Singapore. To qualify for this option, the employer must meet a set of criteria (e.g., capital requirement, excellent past tax records, HR and computer system requirements etc.) and obtain approval from the Singapore Tax authority in advance. In reality, it is burdensome and not easy for many early stage companies to qualify for and execute.

---

27 The tax deferral scheme referred to as the Qualified Employee Equity-based Remuneration (QEEBR) Scheme was introduced by the Singapore authority in 1999.

Special PRC SAFE considerations

The State Administration for Foreign Exchange (or *SAFE*) of the People's Republic of China has jurisdiction over ownership of foreign securities by its citizens. Just like foreign currencies, PRC citizens cannot legally own foreign securities without first registering with SAFE. Because of this restriction, options granted to PRC citizens typically contain additional restrictions on exercisability, ranging from the most draconian (and standard) permutation of a PRC option not being exercisable at all without obtaining SAFE approval, to the more benign permutations of (1) permitting exercise and transfer to eligible holders (e.g., non-PRC relatives of an optionee), (2) setting up a mechanism for quasi-exercise and (3) extending the post-separation validity of a PRC option, etc..

Failing to provide for a mechanism that addresses SAFE restrictions, and thereby permitting PRC optionees to freely exercise and become shareholders of the company without first registering with SAFE, could spell trouble for the company down the road if it ever sets up a subsidiary in China and needs to inject capital or repatriate profit from China. To the extent a startup company is acquired by a sophisticated buyer, any historical lapse in this area also forecloses certain deal structures and spells additional headaches during due diligence and deal execution.

Restricted shares

Another common form of equity incentive instrument is the *restricted share*. In contrast to options, which are contractual rights to acquire stock at some future date at a fixed price, a grant of restricted shares represents an outright grant of stock for no cost (or sometimes for a nominal purchase price) and gives the recipient immediate share ownership and voting rights, which options do not endow on its holders.

The shares are called "restricted" because they are subject to certain limitations (in particular vesting). Because restricted shares are granted outright for no cost or nominal cost, the incentivizing effect of restricted shares is arguably weaker than options, since restricted shares have intrinsic value even without any appreciation in the enterprise value of the startup company.

One other key difference between options and restricted shares is that restricted shares are typically immediately taxable to the recipient as income upon grant. In contrast, options are typically not taxed until the time of exercise (or possibly even later, at the time of sale of the underlying shares).[28]

The different tax treatment between options and restricted shares makes the latter a potentially unappealing award for employees of startup companies because the recipients face the specter of immediate cash outlay for tax payable on receipt of illiquid startup company equity (that may or may not be worth anything in the future). In jurisdictions that mandate employers to withhold taxes payable by employees for compensation, the tax withholding obligation potentially means immediate cash crunch arising from a grant of illiquid equity, which is then a problem not just for the recipients of the restricted shares but for the startup company with a withholding obligation as well.

---

28 For grantees who are U.S. taxpayers, options can be further divided into *incentive stock options* and *non-qualified stock options* based on the intended tax treatment at the time of grant. The timing and rate of tax payable differ accordingly. Startup companies are well-advised to instruct equity award recipients to consult their own personal tax advisors to understand the potential personal tax consequences that may arise from receiving, holding, exercising and ultimately selling an equity incentive award, because each recipient's tax situation will be different.

Restricted share units

A third equity incentive instrument that is a bit of a hybrid between options and restricted shares is *restricted share units*, or *RSUs*. RSUs operate a bit like options in the sense that they represent a contractual right to acquire shares at a later date, subject to the fulfillment of certain conditions, so no shares are immediately issued to the grantee. But RSUs also work like restricted shares in the sense that when the issuance conditions are satisfied, shares underlying the RSUs are issued to the grantee at no cost. Therefore, RSUs share some characteristics with options, including advantageous tax deferral characteristics[29] and some other characteristics with restricted shares, primarily the lack of an exercise price. On the flip side, RSUs also share some of the disadvantages of options and restricted shares,[30] namely, that RSUs do not confer any voting rights to their holders, and the incentivizing effect of RSUs is arguably weaker than options since there is no exercise price payable to receive the underlying shares.

Vesting and other restrictions, revisited

Just as founder shares are typically subject to vesting, such as time-based vesting over a certain number of years, so too are equity incentive instruments granted under ESOP. Unlike founder vesting, though, ESOP awards usually also include what is known

---

29 Another advantage is that, with respect to PRC recipients, since RSUs are not shares, there are no immediate concerns pertaining to SAFE compliance. However, note that for grantees who are U.S. taxpayers receiving RSUs grants from a non-U.S. company, the tax deferred nature of RSUs is severely limited under U.S. tax rules (i.e., only RSUs granted by U.S. companies are fully tax-deferred under U.S. tax laws).

30 In additions, RSUs have a unique disadvantage with respect to vesting conditions, discussed below.

as a "*cliff*," which conceptually is like a probation period for the recipient before any of the underlying shares are vested. The cliff is typically 1 year and is often expressed as "X-year vesting with Y-year cliff" (e.g., 4-year vesting with 1-year cliff, which means the first 25% of the ESOP award will vest after 12 months in a lump sum and the remaining 75% will vest ratably over the subsequent 36 months).

The cliff prevents startup companies from having to issue shares to any employees who did not stay at the company for a meaningful period of time (e.g., one year). In the context of options and RSUs, "vesting" generally means the schedule at which options become exercisable.[31] In the context of restricted shares, "vesting" means that the restricted shares are released from the company's right to buy back the shares at cost or for nominal consideration upon termination of the service provider. In all three cases, "vesting" denotes that the holder's right in the instrument is now fully conferred and cannot be taken away absent certain extenuating circumstances set forth in the governing plan documents.

---

31 Note that RSUs are subject to the additional vesting condition that the company must consummate an initial public offering or sale of the company before a holder's right to receive shares vests. Since the occurrence of such events is entirely out of the recipients' control (and keeping in mind that if the recipient leaves the company, the award lapses after a certain period of time, typically 3 to 7 years), this additional vesting condition represents a huge risk of forfeiture of the RSUs to their recipients. RSUs' idiosyncratic vesting requirement is a byproduct of U.S. tax laws, though observed market practice is to follow such requirements even when U.S. tax laws do not apply, if for no other reason than to ensure that a startup company's ESOP documents/awards look and behave like everyone else's and do not need to be explained to potential investors or acquirers on how and why they work. Also see footnote 32 for cautionary statement on non-U.S. companies granting RSUs to service providers who are U.S. taxpayers.

It is important to note that vesting is not something intrinsically required for ESOP awards (i.e., awards may be granted without any vesting restrictions whatsoever, or "fully vested").[32] Therefore, other vesting arrangements, though rare, are entirely possible. Out of the possible non-time-based arrangements, one of the most frequently seen is performance based vesting. But such vesting schemes are rare for a variety of reasons, the most important being that performance criteria, to the extent that it is set at the individual or team level, tends to incentivize more selfish behavior on the part of the recipients and do less to orient behaviors toward the overall success of the company.

Lastly, as we mentioned in Chapter 1, right of first refusal and lock-up restrictions should be applied to all equity issued from the ESOP.

---

32 With the exception being the IPO/sale of the company vesting conditions for RSUs discussed in the footnote above.

Chapter 3
Funding Overview

Now that the company has been properly set up and thriving, it is ready to go out and seek funding. Let's take a look at what the typical funding process looks like:

Very early stage equity or convertible instrument financing (angel and seed stage)

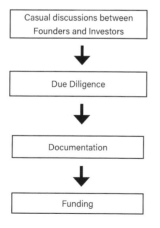

- Minimum due diligence (if at all) is done
- Often only involves checking out company website and reading business plan
- Company provides simple funding documents

Early to middle stage equity financing (Series A, B, C⊠)

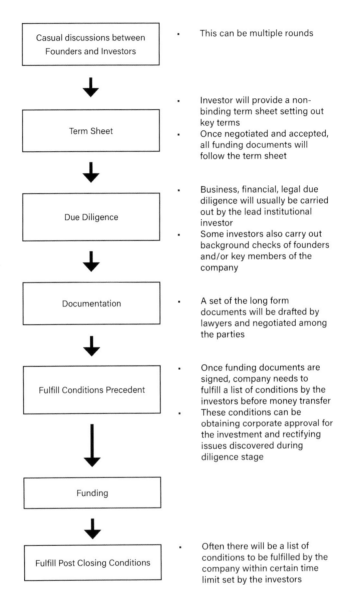

Casual discussions between Founders and Investors
- This can be multiple rounds

Term Sheet
- Investor will provide a non-binding term sheet setting out key terms
- Once negotiated and accepted, all funding documents will follow the term sheet

Due Diligence
- Business, financial, legal due diligence will usually be carried out by the lead institutional investor
- Some investors also carry out background checks of founders and/or key members of the company

Documentation
- A set of the long form documents will be drafted by lawyers and negotiated among the parties

Fulfill Conditions Precedent
- Once funding documents are signed, company needs to fulfill a list of conditions by the investors before money transfer
- These conditions can be obtaining corporate approval for the investment and rectifying issues discovered during diligence stage

Funding

Fulfill Post Closing Conditions
- Often there will be a list of conditions to be fulfilled by the company within certain time limit set by the investors

In the following chapters we will dive into each of these steps in greater detail.

Chapter 4
Due Diligence

For companies seeking funding, due diligence is an unavoidable step they must go through. This chapter aims to shed some light on this often painful and tedious process and to help startup companies navigate through it smoothly.

For very early stage companies and "family and friend rounds" which target to raise only a very small amount of money, the due diligence process is usually informal and less stringent. It may be no more than a few informal chats and/or the review of a few key documents.

Once a company reaches the later stages of financing (e.g., series A onwards), investors typically carry out a thorough due diligence on the company and its founding team. This involves a detailed examination of the company's business, operations, finance, legality, compliance, intellectual property, founding team and if the company is a tech company, its technology, IT systems and software, etc.. The company will be required to answer a comprehensive due diligence questionnaire and deliver supporting documents for scrutiny by the investor and its professional advisors.

Although due diligence is usually carried out when the term sheet is signed and the parties have reached agreement on the key terms of the funding (e.g., valuation, investment amount, liquidation preference, etc.), there can be many obstacles that need to be overcome between the due diligence and the actual funding. Therefore, good corporate governance and record keeping are something the company management needs to take very seriously from the inception of the company with a view that every aspect of the company's business is subject to the future examination by potential investors.

Let's take a closer look at what the due diligence process typically involves.

Business due diligence

For business due diligence, investors seek to have a detailed understanding of the company's business as a whole, including its ownership, business structure, corporate structure, industry, business strategy, operations, assets, products, competitors, associates, distributors, suppliers, customers, and so on.

Supporting documents to be delivered for business due diligence may include:

- corporate structure chart (showing the chain of ownership, joint ventures and affiliates);
- business organization structure chart (identifying departments, directors, management team and key

personnel, etc.);

· business strategy and overview of business and industry;

· lists of assets, products, suppliers, distributors, associates, customers, etc.; and

· contracts with suppliers, distributors, associates, customers, third party service providers, etc..

Founder and human resource due diligence

For startup companies, the founders are the most crucial ingredient in the company's recipe for success and therefore are also the biggest risk factor for the investors. Many institutional investors have an established process to conduct background checks on the founders and the key personnel. This could involve calling the founder's friends, associates, ex-colleagues or industry experts regarding the founder's capability, character, reputation, education background and career history.

To the surprise of many founders, some investors may even engage professional investigation firms to carry out thorough checks on the founders and/or the key personnel. Such background checks often involve detailed examination of education and career history, family and corporate affiliation, in-depth media profile search, litigation/bankruptcy/enforcement/sanction search, regulatory compliance and identification of "red flags" in general.

Founders should be aware that their personal conduct, media profile and general reputation are all under the purview of due diligence. However, it doesn't mean that a company won't be able to raise funding unless its founders have a spotless history and reputation. The investors will examine each case based on its own merits, weighing the risks against various commercial considerations. In an extreme scenario, even a criminal record on the founder could be acceptable to the investor from a business perspective. What's important is that the founder makes an honest and full disclosure upfront.

Other than the founders, the investors may also request for information on the company's employees and service providers, including their scope of responsibilities, turnover rates and HR policies. Often Investors will also request to interview the employees, sometimes on very short notice.

Supporting documents to be delivered for founder and human resource due diligence may include:

- management team list, profile and responsibilities;
- former management team list and reasons for departure;
- employee list, profile and responsibilities;
- employment and service contracts; and
- staff manual.

Financial due diligence

During financial due diligence, investors will closely examine the financial process and control of the company as well as its accounts. Accounting firms are often hired to give an expert opinion and raise "red flags" on the company's financial condition. Details of bank accounts, past rounds of funding and the planned use of proceeds will also need to be disclosed to the investors.

Supporting documents to be delivered for financial due diligence may include:

- financial statements for the last 3 to 5 years;
- management reports;
- accounting standard and policies;
- details of past equity and debt funding rounds;

- bank account details and balances; and
- details of all assets (including fixed assets and IP).

Legal, tax and compliance due diligence

Through this part of the due diligence process, investors seek to establish the legitimacy, legal compliance and good corporate governance of the target business. The legal counsel of the investors will review all corporate records (e.g., company formation documents, licenses, board and shareholder resolutions, minute books, company bylaws, etc.), tax related documents and all material contracts and other documents evidencing obligations that bind the company.

We cannot over-emphasize the importance for the company to consistently keep a good record of all documents in an organized manner. Many early stage companies struggle with compiling and finding corporate documents, resulting in serious delays in the funding process.

Supporting documents to be delivered for legal, tax and compliance due diligence may include:

- company formation documents and bylaws;
- board and shareholder resolutions and minutes;
- business licenses, industry and compliance approvals;
- IDs of shareholders;
- all material contracts binding the company or relating to the company;
- list of present, past and threatened litigations, administrative penalties, arbitration awards (if any);
- insurance policy summary (if any); and
- tax assessment returns and penalties.

Related party transactions due diligence

It is quite common for the founders, shareholders or officers of an early stage company to have business dealings with the company. For example, a major shareholder may be leasing out an office space to the company or a firm which the founder holds a stake in provides IT services to the company. Understandably, from the investors' perspective, they want to make sure that these transactions are carried out at arm's length and not used to funnel money out of the company. The company is required to disclose any dealings with a "related party", such as a shareholder, a founder, a member of the management team or any entity any of them controls or has an interest in.

Supporting documents to be delivered for related party transactions due diligence may include:

- details of all current and anticipated related party transactions; and
- all agreements documenting related party transactions.

Intellectual property/information technology due diligence

For companies that rely heavily on technology and/or IT systems, due diligence will center around their technology, IT systems, software and intellectual properties. Investors often engage experts to examine and test out the technology and systems before reaching an informed judgement.

Supporting documents to be delivered for IP, IT due diligence may include:

- list and description of all IT systems, hardware and software;

- list of all registered and unregistered intellectual properties;
- industry certification of company products (if any);
- detailed technology and product roadmap;
- customer details and data;
- test results, evaluations and data of existing products and products under development;
- details of system and/or product development plan and progress;
- development, configuration management strategy; and
- disaster recovery process and business continuity plan.

Summary

Companies seeking funding should never underestimate the scope of the due diligence process. Investors and their professional advisors will look into every nook and cranny of the company and weigh their finds against their investment risks, including the justifiability of the valuation. Even if the investors, after the due diligence process, reach the decision to fund the company, they often demand the company to, at a minimum, remedy the key risks that the investors have identified during the due diligence process before hitting the button on the wire transfer. Again, good corporate governance and record keeping practices from the inception of the company will help the company greatly when it reaches the funding stage.

Chapter 5
Bridge (Convertible Instruments) Financing

Typically, early stage companies will utilize one of the following vehicles to raise money:

- convertible instruments, which include convertible promissory notes, SAFE and KISS; or
- equity financing, which is a direct subscription of equity in the company.

Valuing an early stage company is usually difficult as it might only have a business plan, some early intellectual properties and perhaps a working prototype with little commercialization or demonstrable traction or income. At this stage it would be hard to attract institutional investors, hence the need to seek funding from friends, family and perhaps angel investors who specialize in investing in very early stage companies.

Few of the likely investors at this stage are equipped to put a valuation on the company (and to be fair, companies at this stage offer very little on which valuation can rationally be based). To kick the can down the road, a popular approach for investments at this stage is to use a convertible instrument, which are debt or equity instruments for a fixed investment amount with a built-in option to convert into equity of the company following the occurrence of a trigger event. Let's take a closer look at each of these convertible instruments.

Convertible promissory note

A convertible promissory note is basically a term loan with a built-in feature to convert the loan amount into equity of the company (typically preferred shares) upon the occurrence of certain triggering events[33]. Like all other loans, if no triggering event occurs by the maturity date, theoretically the loan amount (together with any accrued interest) shall be repaid. However, in most startup cases the money will be spent building the business and there will be no realistic prospect for repayment. Conversion into shares at the next round of financing or upon acquisition of the company are more likely exit options for investors.

The convertible promissory note was until recently the most

---

33 Which may be as simple as the occurrence of a future equity financing meeting certain pre-determined criteria, at which point the conversion of the convertible promissory note into equity may be at the option of the holder automatically or subject to further conditions, depending on how the parties allocate the trigger mechanisms and set up the subsequent decision tree.

commonly used vehicle to structure angel funding. However, with the fast-evolving startup market, new instruments such as SAFE and KISS were introduced to address startup specific issues a convertible promissory note can't address.

SAFE

SAFE stands for "Simple Agreement for Future Equity". It has increasingly become the more favored instrument in the last few years. Unlike a convertible promissory note, SAFE is technically not a debt instrument (i.e., not a loan). Loans have a maturity date and the power of rendering the company insolvent if unpaid upon maturity. Under SAFE, the company's obligation to repay or convert is entirely event-driven, with no burden of maturity or interest. The triggering events for a convertible promissory note and SAFE are largely similar (i.e., next round of financing, sale of company, etc.). It is generally viewed to be more company-friendly than a traditional convertible promissory note.

KISS

KISS stands for "Keep It Simple Security" (not as sexy as it sounds). The original version was created by 500 Startups in 2014 with the intention to, literally, keep it simple. It has become quite popular over time, and we see more and more startups issuing KISS-es in return for funding. KISS comes in two different flavors - debt KISS or equity KISS. There are many subtle differences, but you can generally think of a debt KISS as more similar to a convertible promissory note (except it's shorter and simpler), with debt maturity and interest built in, and an equity KISS as more similar to SAFE, with no debt maturity and interest. As one can imagine, between the two KISS flavors, the equity KISS is more company-friendly.

Advantages of convertible instruments

Given the likely pool of investors (friends, family and early angel investors) and the company's lack of tangible assets and traction on the commercial front, it would be hard to put a valuation on the company. But a valuation of the company is required for the company to issue shares (as we will see in the next chapter) because without a valuation, the company would not be able to figure out how many shares to issue in exchange for a given amount of investment.

To bridge the gap, a convertible instrument may be used. With convertible instruments, the company sidesteps the issue of valuation because no equity is issued – the company simply issues a convertible instrument that says (in the case of a convertible note and debt KISS only) that the company promises to pay back the invested amount by maturity date if conversion to equity does not occur before maturity, or conversion will occur at the triggering event by reference to the valuation at the triggering event.

Another advantage for startup companies fundraising with convertible instruments is that they give the company runway to grow its valuation and diminish the amount of dilution from the investment. This is because the amount of investment is fixed, whereas presumably the company's valuation continues to grow over time – the rate of growth simply has to outpace the rate of interest accrual on the convertible promissory note or debt KISS in order for the company to come out ahead. For this reason, convertible instruments are also disfavored by some institutional venture investors.

Also, since the convertible instruments are simply a debt instrument and/or a right to convert to future equity, it is relatively simple and straightforward. As a result, documentation is much shorter and simpler compared to an equity financing. One reason is because convertible instruments permit companies to sidestep the extensive documentation needed for legislating various shareholder rights upfront because convertible instruments do not grant any shareholder rights at the time of investment.

Thus, convertible instruments are attractive options for very early stage companies as an instrument that let companies punt on the question of valuation and are quick to implement.

Example:

An investor approaches ABC Company wanting to invest $100,000. However, neither ABC Company nor the investor has a clear sense what percentage of ABC Company the $100,000 should buy because neither party knows the *valuation* of ABC Company. In other words, you would have to know that ABC Company's valuation prior to an investment (what is frequently referred to as *pre-money valuation*) is (for example, $900,000) in order to figure out that $100,000 buys 10% of ABC Company. Just to play out this scenario, recall that ABC Company has 2,105,263 total shares including the ESOP, so at a $900,000 valuation, that would translate into $900,000 ÷ 2,105,263 shares = $0.4275 per share. A $100,000 investment would purchase $100,000 ÷ $0.4275 = 233,918 shares. So now ABC Company's capitalization would be, if it accepts the proposed investment, 2,000,000 founder shares + 105,263 ESOP + 233,918 investor shares, totaling 2,339,181 shares. Just to be sure we have done our math right, let's take 2,339,181 x $0.4275 = $999,999.88 (the $0.12 difference is due to rounding).

But let's say you don't think the valuation of ABC Company is merely $900,000, so you are left with two options. You can either continue to negotiate the implied valuation of ABC Company by negotiating the percentage of ABC Company that $100,000 buys (but with neither party having a clear idea how to value ABC Company), or the parties can bypass that entire discussion by using a convertible instrument.

And hopefully, in 6 to 12 months, when ABC Company has better traction and a clearer sense of its own value, it will be talking about a valuation measured in the millions, so the same $100,000 investment ends up with a smaller portion of ABC Company. But why would an investor go for convertible instruments?

Disadvantages of convertible instruments

The first disadvantage of convertible instruments happens to be the advantages covered above: namely, there is no valuation, so it could (gasp!) go down, and that if the instrument is a debt instrument (e.g., convertible promissory note or debt KISS) and not equity, in theory it needs to be repaid by the company. In reality, assuming all the proper corporate formalities have been observed (and that is why we spent some time previously covering the subject), a convertible promissory note or debt KISS is strictly a liability of the company and not the personal liability of the founders. From that perspective, the convertible promissory note and debt KISS are relatively low-risk instruments from a personal liabilities perspective because if the founding team has been diligent about keeping good records and good corporate governance, the chances of incurring personal liability is basically zero.[34]

Nonetheless, a lot of entrepreneurs get an unsettling feeling from any kind of debt, but at the end of the day we must keep in mind that the purpose and intention for the instrument is to one day convert into equity. So, to the extent that the company is one that is fast-growing and anticipates getting interest from institutional investors for equity financing, then it is well situated to do a convertible instrument financing.

---

34 Though in many jurisdictions in Asia, investors are accustomed to asking for and getting the founders to guarantee the debt so they have "skin in the game".

Example:

8 months after getting the $100,000 convertible promissory note funding, ABC Company is not doing so hot, and it's almost out of cash. Now the investor is talking about a $400,000 valuation for ABC Company or repayment on maturity, and you and your co-founder are kicking yourselves for not taking the investment as equity at a $900,000 valuation.*

* Sometimes a decrease in valuation is not just a function of how the company is doing. Those with memories of 1999, 2007 or 2015 will probably remember what happened subsequent to those years. There were plenty of companies that put off valuation, thinking that it's going to be higher in 2000, 2008 or 2016, and we all know what happened afterwards.

Sweeteners, kickers and conversion valuation caps

In exchange for putting off valuation, the quid-pro-quo for the deferral is that investors will typically expect some sort of discount or boost to the amount of equity they will receive when a convertible instrument ultimately converts. This could take the form of a conversion price discount. For example, the convertible instrument issued by the company might say that at the time the convertible instrument converts into the company's equity, it will be done at a discount to the price paid by the investors in that round, which represents the investors' reward for taking an earlier risk on supporting the company.[35]

---

35 It should also be noted that from an investor's perspective, the upside of the convertible instrument is only limited to the discount the instrument carries at conversion unless the parties agree to a valuation cap when the instrument is issued. The topic of valuation cap will be explained in more detail in the next chapter.

Example:

> If ABC Company's $100,000 convertible promissory note stipulates a 20% conversion price discount, and ABC Company's series seed financing is done at $1.00 per share, then the note investor will be entitled to convert the note at $0.80 per share. So instead of receiving 100,000 shares in ABC Company ($100,000 ÷ $1.00), the note investor will instead receive 125,000 shares in ABC Company ($100,000 ÷ $0.80) because of the conversion price discount.

Alternatively, the convertible promissory note may have warrant coverage[36] that stipulates that the investor is entitled to acquire some additional percentage of shares in the company for a nominal price or fixed price.

Example:

> If ABC Company's $100,000 convertible promissory note stipulates an additional 20% warrant coverage for nil consideration, and ABC Company's series seed financing is done at $1.00 per share, then the note investor will be entitled to convert the note at $1.00 per share and, after conversion, receive 20% of additional shares, which works out to $100,000 ÷ $1.00 x 120% = 120,000. So instead of receiving 100,000 shares in ABC Company ($100,000 ÷ $1.00), the note investor will receive 120,000 shares in ABC Company because of the additional warrant coverage. Note that even though the percentage for conversion discount and warrant coverage are both stated as "20%", the results are different.*
>
> *   This is not to say that one method is preferable over the other (as matter of fact, the authors prefer conversion price discount for its

---

36 A *warrant* works pretty much like an option, i.e., an instrument that gives its holder the contractual right to acquire equity from the company at some future date at a pre-determined price and subject to the terms set forth in the warrant.

simplicity – it is simply a paragraph in the convertible instrument, whereas the warrant is an additional document that needs to be drafted and negotiated), but merely that the parties should know the difference and make adjustments accordingly.

Based on the above, it should be plain to see that there is a cost to the various advantages of doing a convertible instrument financing. Another typical feature (though more frequently demanded by institutional investors) for convertible instruments is that, to the extent the company goes public or is acquired prior to there being an equity financing that determines valuation for the company, the investor at that point has a choice of converting the convertible instrument into equity at some fixed price, or the convertible instrument becomes repayable at some multiple of the original face value (typically two to five times the investment amount). This way, the investor is rewarded for its early risk taking and shares in the upside of the company's successful exit.

Example:

ABC Company's $100,000 convertible promissory note stipulates that if ABC Company goes IPO or is sold before there is an equity financing, then the investor may elect to convert the note at $2 million valuation or take 3x repayment. If ABC Company is sold for $2 million, then the investor is better off taking his 3x repayment. If ABC Company is going public or being sold for $1 billion, then conversion becomes a no-brainer (for a staggering 1,000x return on investment)!

Investors will also frequently try to extend the conversion valuation concept from an IPO/exit scenario to any conversion (e.g., stipulating that the convertible promissory note will convert at a 20% discount to the price of the next round, but in any event at no more than $X million pre-money valuation). There are a lot of nuts and bolts involved in negotiating such arrangements that we won't cover here, but fundamentally the concept takes the party back to a negotiation about valuation (albeit in the form of a valuation cap), which somewhat defeats the purpose of doing a convertible instrument in the first place.

We will revisit the topic of these sweeteners, kickers and conversion valuation caps in the next chapter when we look at equity financing term sheet.

Maturity and conversion

Because the intent of the convertible instruments is to sidestep valuation and to utilize a relatively quick and straightforward vehicle to inject capital into the company, what entrepreneurs will want to make sure is that they have enough runway to build value.

Therefore, it would typically not make sense to enter into a convertible promissory note or a debt KISS that has a very short fuse for repayment (e.g., matures in 3 to 6 months) because that would undermine the purpose of delaying valuation. The company should consider asking for anywhere from 12 to 24 months as runway towards an equity financing event, because to the extent the company does not receive equity financing by the maturity date, the amount owned on a convertible promissory note or debt KISS becomes repayable by the company to the investor.

It should also be noted that convertible instruments are sometimes used as a short bridging finance vehicle when the company is very close to confirming the next round of funding but is running out of money in the meantime. In such a scenario, the existing investors may inject capital into the company via convertible instruments and the maturity date for repayment is usually much shorter (e.g., in 3 to 6 months) – just long enough to tide the company over to the next round of funding.

Speaking of conversion at the equity financing event, there are a variety of ways for that to occur. From the investor's perspective, it will want to have control over how and when the convertible instrument converts, and therefore it will want to have the conversion triggered at the sole option and discretion of the investor. Conversely, the company will want the same thing, except at the sole option and discretion of the company. A frequent compromise bridging the gap is that the parties will agree in advance on acceptable parameters for an equity financing (e.g., issuance of shares with gross proceeds of at least $X million dollars), at which point the convertible instrument will automatically convert into equity without either the investor or the company being able to exercise any discretion. It makes sense for both parties to agree in advance on parameters that will define a successful financing at which point neither the investor nor the company has the option of backing out and receiving (repaying) money instead of receiving (issuing) shares.

Chapter 6
Equity (Stock) Financing Term Sheet

In the previous chapter we talked about how an early stage startup may want to sidestep discussion on valuation and instead take advantage of convertible instrument financing. But sooner or later (and for the company's sake, hopefully sooner), the company will have to seek an equity financing and confront the subject of valuation.

In terms of the legal documentation for an equity financing, the first step is to negotiate a term sheet. A number of companies (and a surprising number of investors) will forego seeking professional advice during this stage. But the term sheet is arguably the most important document in the entire process, because it sets forth all the principal terms, rights, preferences and privileges of the stock that's going to be sold by the company. And it is very, very bad form for either party to go back on its words, as embodied by the term sheet.

A typical term sheet is divided into three principal areas covering (1) economic terms, (2) control terms and (3) additional contractual rights of the investor. These three terms are not necessarily so neatly categorized or clustered, but in general it is conceptually helpful to group the various terms into these three broad categories.

Term sheets usually also contain terms governing the purchase itself, as well as a limited number of binding provisions that protect the investor from serving as a mere stalking horse for the company. To help our readers better visualize the discussion, below is a standard "one pager" term sheet that in recent years has become popular with entrepreneurs and investors alike for its brevity and user friendliness.[37]

---

37 Readers interested can compare and contrast the sample with the more traditional (and longer) term sheet, such as the template put out by the National Venture Capital Association (www.nvca. org), which provides a set of annotated financing document templates under "Resources" – "Model Legal Documents" (as of the publication of this book).

Sample "One Pager" term sheet

SERIES SEED PROPOSAL FOR ABC COMPANY
May 31, 202[*]

Closing	On or before [*], 202[*]		
Investment & **Post-Money** **Ownership**	XYZ Fund	$2M	40.0%
	Founders, Team & Prior Investors		40.0%
	Available Option Pool		20.0%
Security	Series Seed Preferred Shares.		
Dividend	8% non-cumulative if and when declared by Board.		
Liquidation **Preference**	Non-participating; **1X** original purchase price plus declared dividends.		
Redemption	After five years; **1X** original purchase price plus declared dividends.		
Conversion	At holder's option and automatically on closing of IPO with at least $20 million of net proceeds to the Company.		
Anti-dilution	Standard adjustments; [broad-based weighted average/ratchet].		
Board	Board to include **1** XYZ Fund Board Member.		
Voting Rights	Approval of majority of the Preferred Stock on standard protective provisions.		
Investor **Rights**	Standard registration, information, preemptive and other customary investor rights [; most favored nation status against terms applicable to [prior/all future] Company issuances].		
Vesting, ROFR **& Co-Sale**	• Four-year monthly vesting with 1 year cliff for all employees • Founder vesting to be mutually agreeable to parties • No transfers except for estate planning • Right of first refusal to Company followed by Investor; co-sale rights for Investor		
Reps & **Warranties**	Standard.		
Closing **Conditions**	Opinion of counsel. Satisfactory completion of due diligence. Standard and customary investor rights, including financial statement, pre-emptive and registration rights. Employees and founders sign proprietary information agreement.		
Legal	Counsel to be mutually agreeable to the parties. Work towards *pari passu* terms wherever possible. The Company will pay reasonable legal fees and expenses incurred by a counsel, subject to a cap of $50,000.		
Expiration	This offer will expire at 5:00 pm Pacific Time on [Friday], [*], 202[*].		

The existence of this proposal and its terms are confidential and shall not be disclosed to a third party except as may be necessary to consummate the financing. From the signing date hereof until the earlier of (i) 5:00 P.M. Pacific Time on [*], 202[*], (ii) the closing or (iii) written notification by XYZ Fund that it does not intend to proceed with the financing, the Company agrees that it shall not solicit, encourage others to solicit, encourage or accept any offer for the purchase or acquisition of any capital stock of the Company, of all or any substantial part of the assets of the Company, or proposals for any merger or consolidation involving the Company and it shall not negotiate with or enter into any agreement or understanding with any other person with respect to any such transaction. Except for the preceding two sentences which the parties agree are legally binding, this proposal is an expression of intention only and does not constitute a legally binding agreement.

_____   _____
on behalf of ABC Company   on behalf of XYZ Fund

Valuation

The first and the most important term focused on by all the businesspeople during the term sheet stage is valuation. How do you value a company, and what are the components to pre-money valuation? We have spent quite a bit of time in previous chapters discussing both the employee stock ownership program as well as sweeteners, kickers and conversion valuation caps promised by the company in connection with the issuance of convertible instruments, and those concepts now all come into play when we talk about a company's pre-money valuation.

The concept of valuation is intuitively straightforward: the investor will (1) assign a value on the company and (2) propose an amount that they will invest into the company. Based on those two numbers, you can then derive the percentage ownership by the investor following the financing.[38] For example, if the company is valued at $3 million, and investor proposes to invest $2 million, then following the investment, the company's valuation will be $5 million, with the investor owning 40% of the company (corresponding to its $2 million investment).

Example:

The term sheet from XYZ Fund is somewhat convoluted by stating that XYZ Fund will invest $2 million for 40% of ABC Company, so in order to figure out the "pre-money valuation", you need to do the math by taking $2 million ÷ 40% to get $5 million total post-investment valuation, which means that the pre-money valuation must be $5 million - $2 million = $3 million.

---

38 Note that for some investors, the amount to be invested is not as important as getting to their target percentage ownership post-financing, so the investment amount becomes the plug number in such investor's equation.

Before we go any further, let's recap the state of ABC Company's capitalization:

Founders (2)	2,000,000 shares (1,000,000 shares each)	95%
ESOP	105,263 shares	5%

$100,000 convertible promissory note, 20% discount, $2 million valuation cap on conversion*

By couching its term sheet in the context of amount of investment / post-investment ownership percentage, XYZ Fund is telling ABC Company that whatever ESOP it had granted previously, whatever discounts and conversion valuation caps it had agreed to previously, those would all be coming out of the founders' ownership and will not impact XYZ Fund's ownership percentage. XYZ Fund has two objectives as implied by its term sheet: (1) own 40% of ABC Company on a *fully-diluted basis*** following its $2 million investment and (2) make sure there is 20% of ABC Company available for future equity incentive grants (because if ABC Company runs out of ESOP and has to increase it, that would dilute all shareholders' ownership percentage, including XYZ Fund's).

Equity Holder	Investment Amount	Shares	% Ownership	% Voting Power***
Founder 1		1,000,000	17.575%	22.4888%
Founder 2		1,000,000	17.575%	22.4888%
ESOP (Old)****		105,263	1.85%	-
ESOP (Available)		1,137,980	20.00%	-

* Recall that ABC Company's angel investor had wanted to invest its $100,000 at $1 million post-investment valuation, but our co-founders successfully pushed the angel investor to do a convertible promissory note instead and pushed off the valuation debate. Now let's assume that the angel investor was successful in getting a $2 million valuation cap not just for IPO and sale of ABC Company, but for conversion as well.

** This term simply means inclusive of all outstanding convertible securities (options, warrants, convertible promissory notes and the like) as well as reserved but unallocated ESOP.

*** Recall that option pool and options do not have any voting power, so those shares are backed out of the denominator for calculating this column.

**** Here, we assume that all 105,263 shares have been allocated and are no longer available, otherwise the available shares can be added to the next row (ESOP Available) and decrease the number of shares that need to be added to ESOP (Available), which results in less dilution to the founders.

Equity Holder	Investment Amount	Shares	% Ownership	% Voting Power***
Angel (Principal Amount)	$100,000	113,798	2.00%	2.5592%
Angel (As a function of Valuation Cap)*	$50,000	56,899	1.00%	1.2796%
XYZ Fund	$2,000,000	2,275,960	40.00%	51.1836%
TOTAL:		5,689,900	100%	100%

The per share price works out to $0.87875. "Pre-money valuation" of $3 million consists of 2,000,000 founder shares, 105,263 shares in the "old ESOP", 1,137,980 shares in the available option pool and a total of 170,697 shares issued to the angel investor for convertible promissory note conversion after applying the conversion valuation cap. 2,000,000 + 105,263 + 1,137,980 + 170,697 = 3,413,940, and multiply that by $0.87875 gives you $2,999,999.78. XYZ Fund's 2,275,960 shares' aggregate value at $0.87875 per share is $1,999,999.85, and so there you have it: $2,999,999.78 + $1,999,999.85 = $4,999,999.63 in post-investment valuation.

This is a purposefully dramatic (though not unprecedented) example to show the cumulative effects of prior decisions, built upon one another over time, that cascade and come to fruition at the time of ABC Company's first equity financing.** Can you identify decisions that could have been made differently that would significantly alter this outcome?

---

*   A couple of points:
1. The conversion valuation cap is more advantageous than the conversion discount of 20%, so the angel receives the former and not the latter. It would be quite unprecedented to have both apply at the same time.
2. In this neat little example, the conversion valuation cap happens to work out to a nice number of "credit" for $50,000 of securities (or, put differently, conversion valuation cap is just a purchase power multiplier calculated from the ratio of the cap and the company's pre-money valuation, which in this case is 1.5x (the ratio between $3 million pre-money valuation and the $2 million conversion valuation cap), and 1.5x of $100,000 is $150,000, with $50,000 being the "credit" to the angel investor (note that the company does not actually receive any cash)); in reality the calculation is frequently an iterative circular calculation that can get quite complex. Here, we can show proof for how the angel investor's share count gives effect to the $2 million conversion valuation cap as follows: $2,000,000 ÷ (1,000,000 + 1,000,000 + 105,263 + 1,137,980 + 113,798 + 56,899) = $0.5858334, and $100,000 ÷ $0.5858334 = 170,697 (which is the same as the total amount being received by the angel investor in our table (113,798 + 56,899 = 170,697).
**   Note that such slight-of-hand is NOT favored by most venture capitalists, because smart investors understand that ultimately the value of the investment rides on a whole lot of hard work by the founders (and a little luck). It is hard enough to make a startup a success to begin with – there is no sense to saddle it with unmotivated founders!

As we see from the illustration above, where the calculation gets tricky is: within the imputed "pre-money valuation" of $3 million and $2 million investment, where do things like the ESOP, the convertible promissory note (and any attendant discount and warrant coverage) go? As you might have already divined from the above, those are topics of heavy negotiation, because the allocation will have a material impact on the founders' and the investors' ownership and voting power.[39]

Other economic terms

Dividend	8% non-cumulative if and when declared by Board.
Liquidation Preference	Non-participating; **1X** original purchase price plus declared dividends.
Redemption	After five years; **1X** original purchase price plus declared dividends.
Conversion	At holder's option and automatically on closing of IPO with at least $20 million of net proceeds to the Company.
Anti-dilution	Standard adjustments; [broad-based weighted average/ratchet].

Apart from valuation, *dividend*, *liquidation preference*, *redemption* and *conversion/anti-dilution* embody the other key

---

39 If, instead of the expression in the sample term sheet of "$2 million for 40% of ABC Company" we have the more typical expression of "$3 million pre-money valuation, $2 million investment", then there would be a lot more negotiation on where various components of the company's capitalization get allocated. For example, the convertible promissory note could very well be considered part of the series seed round investment (just in the form of prepayment). A discussion might be had on whether the discount / conversion valuation discount should be part of the pre-money valuation or part of the series seed round investment. Even the available option pool might be the subject of negotiation over whether it should be a component of ABC Company pre- or post-money valuation.

economic terms of the proposed series seed preferred shares. Dividend is the amount that accrues on the investment during the life of the investment.[40] Liquidation preference is the amount that the investor is entitled to receive prior to all other shareholders of the company in the event of a sale or liquidation of the company (though note that this term typically does not apply to IPOs, which is handled separately). Redemption governs the timing and amount that the investor may demand from the company for the repurchase of such investor's shares at some future date in the absence of an IPO or sale of the company. Conversion, among other uses that we will cover in a subsequent chapter, stipulates terms and conditions for the lapse of the investor's preferential rights. And finally, anti-dilution provides for an adjustment to the investor's ownership of the company in the event the company sells additional shares in the future at a lower price than what the investor paid for its shares. We will cover each of these topics in more detail in a subsequent chapter.

Control terms

Board	Board to include 1 XYZ Fund Board Member.
Voting Rights	Approval of majority of the Preferred Stock on standard protective provisions.

Board and *voting rights* represent the key control terms relating to the investor's investment in the company. As we mentioned in a prior chapter, a company's ultimate decision-making authority (including hiring and firing officers of the company) is vested in its board of directors. Therefore, the composition of the board of

---

40 In the case of *non-cumulative* dividends, dividends do not accrue at all but are merely payable when and if declared by the board of directors of the company.

directors following an equity financing is a topic of keen interest to investors (and so it should be a topic of keen interest to the entrepreneurs as well). In contrast, voting rights cover fundamental changes to a company and/or the rights vested either in the investor's shares or held by the investor that would trigger the requirement for separate approval by the investor (since in vast majority of cases, the investor would not own a majority of the company and therefore is powerless to stop most shareholder actions absent explicit protective provisions that give the investor veto power over such shareholder actions). The exact litany of "standard protective provisions" will be covered in a subsequent chapter.

Investor's rights

Investor Rights	Standard registration, information, preemptive and other customary investor rights [; most favored nation status against terms applicable to [prior/all future] Company issuances].
Vesting, ROFR & Co-Sale	• Four-year monthly vesting with 1 year cliff for all employees • Founder vesting to be mutually agreeable to parties • No transfers except for estate planning • Right of first refusal to Company followed by Investor; co-sale rights for Investor

Investor rights represent principal rights of the investor for its investment into the company. Investor rights are a package of rights detached from the shares themselves and are instead conferred upon and held by the investor for as long as it owns any (or some pre-determined number or proportion of) shares in the company. Out of the terms listed in the sample term sheet, the only one subject to negotiation (and hence bracketed) is the so-called "most favored nation" clause, with the heavily negotiated aspect being whether the clause only looks to past terms or if it covers future issuances as well.

Vesting covers both the standard vesting schedule that the investor expects to be applied to all future company issuances to service providers and the founders' vesting arrangement as well. Standard vesting is rarely controversial, but founder vesting can be a topic of intense negotiation to the extent the investor wants to change the existing vesting schedule, acceleration terms or turn back the clock on ("revest") any already-vested portion of founders' shares. This is possibly something worth fleshing out at the term sheet stage notwithstanding the brevity of the one-page term sheet.

ROFR & Co-Sale are restrictions on founders' shares that serve to protect the investor's interest in the company by handcuffing the founders. This is also a very standard term that we will cover in more detail in a subsequent chapter.

Terms governing the purchase

Reps & Warranties	Standard.
Closing Conditions	Opinion of counsel. Satisfactory completion of due diligence. Standard and customary investor rights, including financial statement, pre-emptive and registration rights. Employees and founders sign proprietary information agreement.
Legal	Counsel to be mutually agreeable to the parties. Work towards pari passu terms wherever possible. The Company will pay reasonable legal fees and expenses incurred by a counsel, subject to a cap of $50,000.

A term sheet will also typically stipulate certain conditions applicable to the transaction itself (as distinguished from the terms for the investment covered above, which are forward-looking and applicable after the deal has closed). Two principal components are representations and warranties by the company in connection with the sale and conditions that must be satisfied before the investor becomes obligated to consummate the transaction and fund the investment. There should be no mystery to these, as conceptually these terms are no different from what one might expect when buying any other large-ticket items, such as a house or a car, or even for renting an apartment (e.g., landlord needs to represent and warrant that heating and plumbing work and renter needs to put down a deposit and first month rent before getting the key (which is the "closing" in such transaction)).[41]

Legal terms cover things like selection of lawyers, allocation of duties and reimbursement by the company of the investor's legal fees. These are all fairly standard features, with the only negotiated term typically being the amount of the company's reimbursement for the investor's expenses.

Binding terms

The existence of this proposal and its terms are confidential and shall not be disclosed to a third party except as may be necessary to consummate the financing. From the signing date hereof until the earlier of (i) 5:00 P.M. Pacific Time on [*], 202[*], (ii) the closing or (iii) written notification by XYZ Fund that it does not intend to proceed with the financing, the Company agrees that it shall not solicit, encourage others

---

41 Though entrepreneurs and investors should think about *who* should stand behind the representations and warranties; it is not uncommon for deals in Asia to require the founding team to give full or limited guarantee for the company's representations and warranties, though in doing so it undermines the limited liability protection afforded by the corporate entity form.

to solicit, encourage or accept any offer for the purchase or acquisition of any capital stock of the Company, of all or any substantial part of the assets of the Company, or proposals for any merger or consolidation involving the Company, and it shall not negotiate with or enter into any agreement or understanding with any other person with respect to any such transaction. Except for the preceding two sentences which the parties agree are legally binding, this proposal is an expression of intention only and does not constitute a legally binding agreement.

Even though the importance and complexity of the term sheet cannot be overemphasized, we have merely scratched the surface. The long form documents will be the ultimate legally binding documents and are typically anywhere from 10 to 20 times the length of the term sheet. For that reason, a term sheet is only an expression of interest and is typically not legally binding.

Nonetheless, there would typically be certain binding terms (as we saw in the sample term sheet) such as confidentiality and exclusivity provisions. The former is self-explanatory, and the latter subjects the company to exclusive negotiation (or sometimes referred to as "no-shop") with the investor for a certain period of time. The purpose of these provisions is so that once a term sheet is signed and the investor allocates resources toward consummating the deal, the investor does not have to worry about the company speaking to others to try to get a better deal (through active solicitation or otherwise).

Therefore, exclusivity is a standard provision in any institutional investor's term sheet and the negotiation around exclusivity is not so much the existence of it but rather the duration during which the company will be bound, as the company has an interest to make sure that the investor either closes the transaction and funds the company, failing which the company is free to move on after a certain period of time to talk to others and not be perpetually locked into dealing with just one investor.

Chapter 7
Funding Documentation Roadmap

Congratulations, you have signed the term sheet, survived the due diligence process and are now ready to enter the documentation stage of the funding.[42] For very early stage fund raising, funding documents are usually very simple. If the fund is raised through a convertible instrument, a simple convertible note, SAFE or KISS will do the trick.[43] Or if the angel investor is subscribing for the ordinary

---

42   Please refer to the chart set out in Chapter 3 for the steps of the funding process.
43   Please refer to Chapter 5 for a detailed discussion on convertible instruments.

shares of the company directly, a short share subscription agreement will be signed. On the other hand, documentation for later rounds of funding (i.e., Series A onwards) gets significantly more complicated, especially when institutional investors are involved. This chapter aims to provide both founders and investors a bird's eye view over the jungle of legal documentation.

Share purchase agreement

Depending on the jurisdiction, this document may be referred to as the share purchase agreement, stock subscription agreement or the share subscription agreement. This agreement reflects the terms and the mechanism of the share purchase according to the term sheet. It sets out the price, the type and the number of the shares to be purchased, representations and warranties given by the company and the investors, covenants (i.e., promises by the company to do or not do certain things), conditions precedent to the consummation of the transaction and conditions subsequent to funding.

Memorandum and articles of association

Depending on the jurisdiction, this document is also called the company constitutional document, the bylaws or in the United States, the articles of incorporation or the certificate of incorporation. The memorandum and articles of association are first adopted when the company is incorporated and binds all members of the company[44].

When new investors become members of the company by subscribing for a new class of preferred shares, the memorandum and articles of association need to be modified to reflect the

---

44 In certain jurisdictions such as Singapore, companies do not have memorandum of association, only articles of association.

economic terms and voting/control terms we saw at the term sheet stage. The key economic terms which need to be added into or redrafted in the memorandum and articles of association include dividend, liquidation preference, conversion, anti-dilution adjustment and redemption provisions. The control related terms are rules governing board composition, election of directors and special protective provisions for the investors.

In many jurisdictions, the memorandum and articles of association are a public document. This adds another layer of protection for the investors as it also serves as a notice to third parties concerning their rights over the company.[45]

Shareholders agreement

The last bucket of terms, mirroring the term sheet, fall into what we would generally call investors' rights, which are contractual rights set forth in one or more documents. For transactions in Asia, these terms are typically set forth in a shareholders agreement or split between a shareholders agreement and a right of first refusal and co-sale agreement. For U.S. deals, typically there would be three agreements: an investors' rights agreement, a right of first refusal and co-sale agreement and a voting agreement. The exact division of terms into one, two or three separate agreements is both a function of market practice/inertia, as well as from trying to strike a balance between minimizing the number of documents versus minimizing the number of signatories (and future signatories) to each document for both ease of administration and confidentiality considerations.

There are a few reasons for these rights being set forth in contract rather than the memorandum and articles of association. First, the contractual rights are sometimes limited to a particular

---

45   But see discussions under Shareholders Agreement below.

group of shareholders or even a particular group of investors, and in those cases it may not be appropriate for such rights to go into the company's memorandum and articles of association, which apply generally to all shareholders. Second, contracts may be amended with just the consent of the signatories (or a subset of the signatories to the extent agreed upon in the document) and do not require the company to go through the formal process typically required by applicable corporate law, such as holding a shareholders' meeting and providing adequate advance notice of such meeting. Third, companies and investors sometimes want to keep the terms of the agreement within a relatively small group of signatories and not generally available to all shareholders (or to any interested parties such as business reporters for companies incorporated in a jurisdiction where constitutional documents are publicly available).

These contractual rights typically include:

- the right for investors to cause the company to register their securities;
- the right for investors to request and receive information on the company;
- preemptive rights by investors to subscribe their proportional portion of any new securities issuances by the company; and
- right of first refusal and co-sale against sale of shares by certain other shareholders of the company.

Founder share restriction deed

As founders are the most essential part of the business, investors want to make sure founders have sufficient incentives to commit to the company long term. However, different from options granted under ESOP, founder shares are issued upfront, sometime without any vesting requirements. This means the founder can leave the company at any time while still holding on to his or her stake. To address this issue, investors customarily require the founder to sign a founder share restriction agreement. This agreement creates a "reverse vesting" on the shares already owned by the founder. The vesting period is usually similar to the one applicable to ESOP (e.g., 4 years (but typically without the 1 year cliff)), during which time, the company or its assignees[46] have the right to purchase the unvested founder shares at a pre-agreed price.

Confidential information and inventions agreement

This agreement is known by many names: the proprietary information and inventions agreement, the confidentiality and inventions assignment agreement, the proprietary information agreement or the protection of company interest agreement, etc.. Whatever name it goes by, the purpose of this agreement is essentially to:

- ensure that all intellectual and industrial properties created by the service provider during the course of employment belong to the company;
- bind the service provider to a covenant to keep the employer's proprietary information confidential and use it only to further the employer's interests;
- grant the company a license to use and sublicense any intellectual properties owned by the service provider

---

46 In many jurisdictions, there are restrictions on companies to buy back their own shares, such as liquidity and notice requirements. In such jurisdictions, it is recommended to build flexibility into the founder share restriction agreement to allow the company to assign its repurchase right to another person or entity.

but used or incorporated by the service provider in the company's products or services;

- in jurisdictions that permit this restriction, limit the scope of competition after the worker leaves the company for a fixed period of time;
- prevent solicitation of any current employee by the service provider to leave the company; and
- make the service provider return company material upon termination of working relationship.

For obvious reasons, the company should make all of its employees and contractors sign this agreement upfront. However, as most of the early stage companies do not take this important step, investors typically require all present and past founders, employees and contractors to execute this agreement as one of the funding conditions.

For early stage companies, it is also common that the founders created the intellectual and/or industry property before they formed the company. In such cases, the intellectual and/or industry property technically belongs to the founder, not the company. It is crucial for the investors to make sure the founders assign all such intellectual and/or proprietary property to the company to avoid the situation whereby the company's core technology and business depends on a piece of intellectual property that it doesn't own. Additional documents such as the deed of IP assignment and the deed of waiver of moral rights are designed to achieve this purpose, under which, the creator of such intellectual property assigns the intellectual property to the company and waives all his or her moral rights relating to the same.

Disclosure schedule

In the share subscription agreement, the company makes certain representations and warranties in relation to various aspects of its business and conditions. To the extent the company's state of affairs deviate from these representations, the company needs to list them out in detail in a disclosure schedule. As failure to disclose renders the company liable for any damages the investors suffer as a result (including diminution in the value of their investment), this is one of the most important documents the company needs to focus on. Further explanation on the disclosure schedule is covered in a later chapter.

ESOP documents

We have discussed the ESOP (employee stock ownership plan) in detail in Chapter 2. Some startup companies have this formally set up before they hire their first employee, but most do not have formal ESOP documents in place until a later stage. In any case, most institutional investors want to make sure the company adopts written ESOP documents when they reach the Series A stage. For this reason, ESOP documents in a form acceptable to the investor is usually a condition precedent to funding.

Management rights letter

As part of the funding document package, some venture capital funds may require the company to sign a management rights letter. In this letter, the company typically grants additional "management rights" to the venture capital fund. These rights include the right to attend company board meetings, access to company financial information and the ability to advise and consult with company management.

The origin of this document is that U.S. venture funds with

U.S. pension plans as their investors request for these rights in order to take advantage of the exemptions under the Employee Retirement Income Securities Act in the United States (commonly known as *ERISA*). Without the exemption, the fund would be subject to various burdensome requirements, limitations, and fiduciary duties imposed by ERISA. Even if the venture fund is not based in the United States, as long as it has U.S. pension plans as investors of the fund (which is often the case) or has the possibility of having U.S. pension plans as investors in the future, the effect of ERISA is something a fund cannot afford to ignore.

Chapter 8

Share Purchase Agreement

I t might be surprising to learn that the share purchase agreement[47], which governs the mechanics for the actual sale of securities, does not contain a whole lot of moving parts governing future events. This is because this agreement is largely intended to be a snapshot in time (or a relatively short period of time between signing and closing), unlike other documents that will have a continuing effect until the company's exit via IPO or sale (and sometimes beyond).

If we were solely concerned with the mechanics of the sale, the share purchase agreement could be a mere two- or three-page document stating that: (1) the company commits

---

47 Readers interested in seeing a sample full version of this document can visit the National Venture Capital Association (www.nvca.org).

to deliver a set number of shares, (2) the investor commits to pay a certain price for such shares and (3) the parties set a time and place where that would happen.

But the share purchase agreement is typically a 15 to 20 page or longer document. What else is covered?

Closing(s)

It is not unusual for a share purchase agreement to provide for multiple closings for a variety of reasons. Sometimes a round of financing will have multiple investors who do not move at the same pace. Sometimes one or more future closings are provided to obligate the company to issue, or the investor to purchase, more shares if certain conditions are met. On some other occasions multiple closings are provided simply because the committed investors are investing an aggregate amount that falls short of the company's target, so the remaining portion is left open for future as-of-yet identified investors.

In any event, the company and the investors largely have their interests aligned on not having subsequent closings that are too far off in the future[48], because the company's valuation will ideally increase over time, and to provide for subsequent closings occurring 6 to 12 months into the future at the same price they are sold today would send the wrong signal regarding the company's own projection about its future valuation and worse yet, become a self-fulfilling prophecy.

Representations and warranties

The meatiest part of the share purchase agreement is typically representations and warranties given by the company to the investor in connection with the sale of securities. The

---

48 90 to 120 days of subsequent closing period is the norm.

representations and warranties serve two purposes. One, if the representations and warranties are incorrect, the investor will have certain remedies against the company. Two, the representations and warranties, in totality, represent the ideal state of a company, and to the extent there are dents and scratches, the company can disclose them in a *disclosure schedule* or *schedule of exceptions* so that the company is not responsible for such exceptions to the ideal state of affairs, and the investor gets a clear idea of existing and potential risks and/or can ask for remedial undertakings by the company.[49]

Corporate Status, Approvals and Capitalization

The litany of representations and warranties given by the company begins with the company representing that it has been properly incorporated, the requisite corporate approvals have been obtained for all the actions being undertaken in connection with the transaction, and that undertaking the transaction will not contravene the company's charter documents. These are the most fundamental representations and warranties present in almost every transaction (not just fundraising transactions), and every company is expected to be able to make these representations and warranties without material exceptions. Put differently, a company that has trouble making these representations and warranties has fundamental issues that will most likely prevent an investment being made if the underlying issue is not corrected.

---

49 If the lapses are significant, there is always a chance the investor pulls the plug on the deal, so it is important to identify known, significant defects early in the cycle to avoid both sides wasting significant time and resources. Being forthcoming on significant issues (in consultation with legal advisors) is always preferable to hiding them, and as the old adage goes, the cover up is worse than the crime, carrying far more significant consequences.

On top of the fundamental warranties discussed above, which are inward looking, the company will also represent and warrant that, externally, the company undertaking the proposed transaction will not trigger any default or other adverse consequences under applicable laws or judgments applicable to the company, with respect to any government authorities having jurisdiction over the company or under any contracts to which the company is bound. The last thing the investor wants to see is that as a consequence of the investment, the company would violate applicable laws[50], lose government licenses or incur additional obligations or penalties under a company contract.[51]

Finally, the last set of representations and warranties in this category deals with the securities issued to the investor and the ownership percentage that would be represented by such securities. After all, the parties will have spent copious amount of time negotiating valuation and ownership percentage, and so it makes sense for the investor to have coverage in the form of representations and warranties to make sure it receives its due benefit. In the capitalization representation, or *cap rep* as it's commonly referred, the company discloses all of its outstanding securities, whether they are stock, options, warrants, convertible promissory notes or other convertible securities, and all other rights to acquire securities from the company, including reserved but unallocated ESOP. In short, anything and everything that may potentially impact the investor's percentage ownership in

---

50 In particular, if the sale of shares is made in the United States or to U.S. buyers, U.S. securities law would apply, and the company as an issuer of securities would need to comply with all the relevant U.S. securities laws, rules and regulations.

51 A myriad of circumstances under which these scenarios would be triggered are beyond the scope of this book, but this reinforces the importance of having good records and documentation as we covered in the first chapter.

the company get fleshed out in the cap rep, so that the investor has a full picture on not only their ownership percentage in the company immediately following the financing, but also contingent events that may impact their ownership percentage.

Taken together, these representations and warranties basically amount to a statement by the company that it exists, has obtained all approvals to do the financing, doing the financing will not get the company in trouble, and after the financing the investor will own X% of the company. These are things that are reasonably expected to be within the company's full knowledge and control.

Financial statements and other operational representations

The next general category of representations and warranties deals with operations and other various "state of affairs" of the company itself and primarily revolves around two concepts, assets and liabilities. The keystone representation here is the financial statements representation (or the *financials rep*), which tells the investor three things: (1) recites and affirms the financial statements that have been provided for due diligence (e.g., for the years ending December 31, 2018 and 2019), (2) states that such financial statements fairly reflect the financial condition and results of the company and (3) states which accounting rules were used to prepare the financial statements, that such rules were applied consistently and whether any of the financial statements are audited. The financials rep assures the investor that the company stands behind the assets and liabilities, income statement and cash flow numbers and related disclosures, if any, provided to the investor in due diligence.

To the extent the company does not have any financial statements, the company would then be asked to give the investor a representation that the company does not have any material liabilities, in lieu of the financials rep (and doing so would then require the company to schedule out its material liabilities on the disclosure schedule, which, while tedious, is exactly the purpose of such representation).

In addition to the financial statements/no material liabilities representations, investors are also commonly interested in specific areas of potential liabilities, which would each be covered by a separate representation and warranty. These include litigation, compliance with laws, tax, employee benefits and retirement funding, environmental concerns, etc.. A well-prepared financial statement theoretically covers all of these (at least the ones that can be quantified), but the reality is that investors know that startups typically do not have financial statements prepared with the same rigor as large public companies, but in any event investors want to know the qualitative details of these liabilities.

Material contracts, which embody a great deal of a company's business and conditions (and by extension, its financial statements), constitute another area which the company will be asked to represent and warrant. Typically, investors will want the company to disclose contracts under which the company's rights or obligations exceed a certain threshold dollar amount or pursuant to which the company might incur any contingent rights or liabilities (e.g., indemnification obligations, guarantees, etc.). For startups, this set of representations and warranties is designed to flesh out the company's major expenditures (e.g., office lease, major supplier and vendor contracts, loan agreements, etc.), corroborate revenues shown on the income statement (e.g., customer agreements, invoices, etc.) and shed light on major restrictions and dependencies (e.g., inbound licenses for key technologies, exclusivity arrangements, material restrictions on conduct of business, etc.).

Share Purchase Agreement

On the assets side of the ledger, investors are almost invariably most interested in the intellectual property of technology companies. For most startups, real estate and other tangible assets often take a backseat to the intellectual property of the company (because intellectual properties represent both a barrier to entry as well as fuel for future growth of the company – think operating system for Microsoft, search engine for Google, database for Oracle), and this harkens back to our discussion at the very beginning of the book about protecting the integrity of the company's intellectual property. In the share purchase agreement, we finally see the importance of intellectual property protection and ownership manifested in an customarily extensive set of representations and warranties, and having done the right things as described in the first chapter will go a long way in ensuring that the company will be able to give the requested representations and warranties without too much problem. In addition to ownership, investors also typically look for a non-infringement representation from the company.[52]

The other big bucket of "assets" of the company is its employees, and investors usually will ask the company to represent and warrant that the company's employees have all signed the requisite contracts (as discussed in the first chapter) and that the company is not aware of its employees planning to go on strike,

---

52 A company may have valid claims to all of the intellectual properties that it has created and may have also taken very good care of protecting such intellectual properties, but if the field covered by the intellectual properties is already subject to some third party's patent, then the company will not be able to commercialize its intellectual properties without potentially infringing such third party's patent. The non-infringement representation is designed to address such a situation and allocate the risk to the company. This may sound unfair to the company, but we will discuss below various techniques to mitigate.

leave the company or otherwise being subject to any conditions or restrictions that would prevent them from devoting their full effort to the company.

Qualifiers – knowledge and materiality

As one might infer from the foregoing discussions, representations and warranties can be broadly categorized into two types, ones in which the company has perfect information (or at least, better information than anyone else) and ones in which the company has imperfect information because the information is not available without undue efforts (such as cataloging all the patents in the world so the company can say with confidence that it does not infringe any of them) or such information is simply unknowable to the company (such as an employee planning to resign).

Tempering the scope of the company's representations and warranties can be done with what is known as a *"knowledge qualifier"*, which basically says that the company is only responsible for the state of affairs to its knowledge (though sometimes the knowledge qualifier itself is modified with further requirements such as the requirement to conduct internal and/or external investigations). This is especially useful for matters such as infringement of third parties' rights or actions of third parties not yet taken or otherwise unknown to the company.

A different sort of qualifier of representations and warranties is what is known as a *"materiality qualifier"*. Materiality is sometimes defined by a dollar threshold, but more frequently it is just left undefined unless and until there is a dispute, at which point it would be up to the court/arbitrator to decide whether a breach rises to the level of being material. A materiality qualifier is helpful for bringing focus to the disclosure schedule on only material items instead of material disclosures being drowned out in a sea of noise.

There is a time and place for one or the other qualifier (and rarely, both) being applied to a particular representation and warranty. While the company is expected to make unqualified representations and warranties about its corporate status, internal approvals and capitalization, on the operational representations and warranties, there is more room for negotiation. Keep in mind though that sometimes investors will not permit the company to qualify certain representations and warranties with knowledge/materiality qualifier, arguing that it unreasonably shifts the risk over to the investor.

Disclosure schedule/schedule of exceptions

As we have alluded to above, both the company and the investors have an interest in the company producing a disclosure schedule/schedule of exceptions to the company's representations and warranties. From the company's perspective, such a document sets forth the exceptions to the representations and warranties, with the effect being the company will not be liable for any items disclosed on the schedule.

From investors' perspective, such a document gives deeper insight into the business and conditions of the company and allows investors to make an informed decision on whether to proceed with the investment. Because of this, the importance of the disclosure schedule cannot be overstated. It is worth reiterating that, absent explicit contrary language, anything disclosed on the disclosure schedule *is not considered a breach*, and so at the time of any financing, it is worthwhile for the founding team to spend the time necessary to ensure that all potential liabilities and lapses in representations and warranties are set forth on the disclosure schedule. From investors' perspective, the objective would be the opposite, meaning that investors have a strong interest in making sure that the disclosure schedule contains very concrete and identifiable disclosures and not an "everything but the kitchen sink" approach that basically eviscerates the bulk of representations and warranties contained in the share purchase agreement.[53]

Remedies

As one might expect, the responsibility for the accuracy of representations and warranties is principally borne by the company. However, it is a widespread practice in Asia for investors to ask the founding team to stand behind the company's representations and warranties and sign on to the share purchase agreement as warrantors. This means that to the extent the company's representations and warranties are inaccurate, in addition to being able to sue the company for damages, investors would have the option to sue the founding team as well. This is of course contrary to the whole point of starting a company to take advantage of the limited liability nature of the corporate entity form, but such is the state of the market due to Asia being relatively new for venture investments, and the higher incidence of fraud and other intentional acts perpetrated during the early days of these markets.

In the event of a breach (or an indemnification obligation being triggered), the company's obligation for damages and indemnification would be unlimited in the sense that all its

---

53 For example, against the intellectual properties representation, the company may "disclose" that "the company may not have all of the intellectual properties it needs in order to conduct its business." A disclosure like this is too ambiguous. What does the company not have? Enough copies of Microsoft Word? Or none of the intellectual properties that was presented in the PowerPoint presentation to the investors? This disclosure, if accepted by investors, basically guts the intellectual properties representations and warranties.

available assets are fair game. With respect to founders, there can be several different permutations with respect to capping their liability. If no limits were set on the founders' exposure as warrantors of the company's representations and warranties, then the default rule is all personal assets of the founders can be claimed against by the investor to cover damages. However, founders can limit their exposure by stipulating, as an example, that their liability for damages is limited to the value of their shares in the company (with the worst case scenario of turning over their shares in the company to the investors). The bottom line is that the guiding principle for founders in these sorts of mitigating clauses is to uphold the contours of the legal theory that corporations are limited liability entities, and founders' other assets outside of the company really should not be put at risk for pursuing their startup dream (absent, of course, fraud or intentional misconduct).[54]

Closing conditions

As we covered in the term sheet discussion, fulfillment of the company's and the investor's respective obligations is also subject to certain conditions (typically referred to as *closing conditions* or *condition precedents* or *CPs*) being met by the company and the investor for the other party's obligation to mature. These items are typically found towards the back of a share purchase agreement.

On the company's part, CPs would typically include items such as restructuring the company such that the holding structure

---

54 There are a whole host of other potential permutations for limiting founders' liability, such as having the company being first in line for claims and repayment before the investors can go after founders for any shortfall, as well as various mechanisms for valuing the founders' shares for the purpose of covering any damages. For hot companies in Asia, founders sometimes manage to negotiate deductibles and dollar caps on their liability for breach of representations and warranties.

and the various local subsidiaries necessary for operations are set up in a way that is agreeable to the investors, the representations and warranties of the companies being true and correct, and covenants and undertakings that are to be performed by the company prior to the closing having been completed. The company will also be responsible for delivering various documents that set forth investor rights that are outlined in the term sheet, as well as other purely transaction-related documents such as a legal opinion and closing certificates. Other closing conditions that are fairly market standard include satisfactory due diligence by the investors and approval of the investment by the investors' investment committees.

In contrast, investors' CPs are typically far more straightforward, with the most important ones being the investors having duly executed and delivered all documents and paying the purchase price for the shares.

Chapter 9

Memorandum and Articles of Association

The economic terms and voting/control terms we saw at the term sheet stage are manifested in the company's memorandum and articles of association[55]. Once the valuation (and hence the ownership in the company) has been set forth in the share purchase agreement (i.e., $X buys Y% of the company, implying a post-investment valuation of $Z), the other terms governing the economic terms of the investment are the dividend, liquidation preference, conversion, and anti-dilution adjustment and redemption provisions, which are all contained in the memorandum and articles of association[56].

---

55 In certain jurisdictions such as Singapore, companies do not have memorandum of association, only articles of association.

56 Readers interested in seeing a sample full version of this document can visit the National Venture Capital Association (www.nvca.org).

Before we dive in, also covered in the memorandum and articles of association are provisions governing board composition, election of directors and special protective provisions afforded to the investor. We will cover those after our discussions of the economic terms.

Dividend

Dividend, in the context of startups, does not share the same conceptual framework as dividend for mature companies. For mature companies with positive cash flow but slow growth, recurring dividend payments represent the bulk of investors' return on investment. In contrast, the notion of a dividend for startup companies really serves as a differentiator between preferred shares and ordinary shares[57] and as a hurdle rate that discourages founders and management from making distributions to shareholders.

Example:

ABC Company had $500,000 of profit in the year following XYZ Fund's investment. You and your co-founder figure a distribution would be a pretty nice year-end bonus, especially for the below-market salary that you have been making. However, your lawyer informs you that because of the 8% preferred dividend, $160,000 would need to be paid to XYZ Fund first (8% on its $2,000,000 investment), and the remaining $340,000 would then be split up proportionately among all shareholders. After doing the math, you realize that you and your co-founder would each get roughly 22.5% of the $340,000, or $76,500 (before taxes). While it's not chump change, it's also not the 6-figure payday you had in mind. So instead, you decide to hold a nice(r) holiday party for the team, give yourselves a bit of a raise for the coming year and pile the rest into a bigger marketing budget.

---

57 This is primarily driven by U.S. tax considerations, which are beyond the scope of this book.

Recall from the term sheet discussion that the above scenario was characterized as *non-cumulative dividends*, which means the company has no obligation to pay or accrue any dividend amount unless the board decides to declare or accrue dividend for the company's shareholders. A contrasting implementation is what is called a *cumulative dividend*, which means regardless of whether a dividend is actually declared or paid by the board, the amount accrues on the company's books and is payable when the company liquidates or is sold. Unlike non-cumulative dividend arrangements, whose purpose is principally one of deterrence, cumulative dividend arrangements are intended to juice the investor's return on investment. Cumulative dividend is further divided into two varieties: dividend carrying simple interest, or dividend carrying compound interest, as we illustrate below:

Example:

> If ABC Company had signed up to cumulative dividend, then regardless of whether ABC Company declares or pays any dividend, a dividend amount would be accrued on XYZ Fund's investment. Assuming ABC Company is sold 5 years after XYZ Fund's investment, at 8% simple interest cumulative dividend, XYZ Fund would be entitled to an extra $800,000 of payment out of the sale proceeds. If XYZ Fund were entitled to 8% compounding interest cumulative dividend, then XYZ Fund would be paid an extra $938,656 out of the sale proceeds.

One exception to the cumulative dividend scenario is when the shares held by the investor convert into ordinary shares (more on conversion below), any previously accrued dividend will be forfeited absent explicit arrangement to the contrary in the memorandum and articles of association.

Liquidation preference

Preference

The most critical term determining return on investment for the investor (and by extension, the founders) in vast majority of startups (in light of IPOs being exceptions rather than the rule when it comes to exits for startups) is the liquidation preference provision. Conceptually, liquidation preference means when a company is liquidated or sold[58], before any amount is distributed to holders of ordinary shares or other junior securities of the company, an amount is first set aside and distributed to investors as holders of preferred shares. One prevailing view of liquidation preference is that it is in essence downside protection for investors. From that perspective, the typical arrangement for liquidation preference is that investors will receive 100% (*"1x"*) of their original investment. However, liquidation preference can also be used to boost return on investment for investors, so we do see in some markets prevalence of 150% (*"1.5x"*) or even 200% (*"2x"*) liquidation preference for investors.[59] Philosophically, that type of arrangement becomes more about guaranteed return on investment desired by the investor and departs from the fundamental notion of liquidation preference being downside protection.

---

58 This is typically referred to as a *deemed liquidation* or *liquidation event* and covers transactions spanning merger and acquisition of the company, sale of all or substantially all assets, change of voting control of the company, and other events negotiated between the company and the investors (though it is extremely rare to include IPOs).

59 Over hundreds of venture financings, the authors have seen a 3x liquidation preference maybe once.

Participation

The term *"participation"* denotes the scenario after setting aside the preference amount for investors, the remaining amounts are allocated among shareholders. There are several permutations for how that might occur. One approach that is the most founder-favorable is that after the preference amount has been set aside, any remaining proceeds are distributed solely to holders of ordinary shares.[60] This approach is consistent with the notion that preference is downside protection, because the investors have to choose between getting their preference or their proportional share of the sale proceeds, but not both.

Before we go any further, below is the baseline example illustrating an exit scenario.

Example:

ABC Company receives an acquisition offer for $5 million (i.e., exactly the post-investment valuation after the series seed preferred shares financing). Here is the breakdown of proceeds to shareholders:

Equity Holder	Shares	% Ownership	Preference	Remainder
Founder 1	1,000,000	17.575%		$878,750
Founder 2	1,000,000	17.575%		$878,750
ESOP*	1,243,243	21.85%		$1,092,500
Angel	170,697	3.00%	$150,000**	
XYZ Fund	2,275,960	40.00%	$2,000,000	
TOTAL:	5,689,900	100%	$2,150,000	$2,850,000

*   Any unissued shares in the ESOP would not be entitled to any distribution, and such unclaimed amount would be allocated among the other shareholders.

**   Recall that the angel investor had the benefit of $2 million conversion cap and as a result received 50% more series seed preferred shares. This sweetener/conversion cap now manifests itself as a 50% boost to the angel investor's liquidation preference.

---

60   This is the meaning of *non-participating* in the term sheet.

Now to illustrate the points we covered above, let's look at the scenarios below.

Example:

ABC Company receives an acquisition offer for $10 million (i.e., exactly 2x the post-investment valuation after the series seed preferred shares financing). Here's the breakdown of proceeds to shareholders:

Equity Holder	Shares	% Ownership	Preference	Remainder
Founder 1	1,000,000	17.575%		$2,420,417
Founder 2	1,000,000	17.575%		$2,420,417
ESOP	1,243,243	21.85%		$3,009,166
Angel	170,697	3.00%	$150,000	
XYZ Fund	2,275,960	40.00%	$2,000,000	
TOTAL:	5,689,900	100%	$2,150,000	$7,850,000

Obviously, this scenario makes zero sense for XYZ Fund, which is just getting back its original investment.* So in reality, a holder of *non-participating preferred shares* would be incentivized (in this scenario) to take its proportional share of the proceeds instead of taking its liquidation preference:

Equity Holder	Shares	% Ownership	Preference	Remainder
Founder 1	1,000,000	17.575%		$1,757,500
Founder 2	1,000,000	17.575%		$1,757,500
ESOP	1,243,243	21.85%		$2,185,000
Angel	170,697	3.00%	$0	$300,000
XYZ Fund	2,275,960	40.00%	$0	$4,000,000
TOTAL:	5,689,900	100%	$0	$10,000,000

* Unless XYZ Fund had negotiated some kind of cumulative dividend, but even then, it would still pale in comparison to the proportional share that XYZ Fund would be entitled to in the example immediately below.

The other possible arrangement is that after setting aside the liquidation preference of the investors, the remaining sale proceeds are distributed among all shareholders, *including the investors*, proportionally based on share ownership.

Example:

ABC Company receives an acquisition offer for $10 million. Here's the breakdown of proceeds to shareholders if investors negotiated 1x liquidation preference *plus* participation:

Equity Holder	% Ownership	Preference	Remainder	Total
Founder 1	17.575%		$1,379,637.50	$1,379,637.50
Founder 2	17.575%		$1,379,637.50	$1,379,637.50
ESOP	21.85%		$1,715,225	$1,715,225
Angel	3.00%	$150,000	$235,500	$385,500
XYZ Fund	40.00%	$2,000,000	$3,140,000	$5,140,000
TOTAL:	100%	$2,150,000	$7,850,000	$10,000,000

Versus the *non-participating* scenario, XYZ Fund receives $5,140,000 (instead of $4,000,000) and the angel investor receives $385,000 (instead of $300,000), a substantial boost to their respective returns.

And just for giggles, let's look at a scenario that combines 1.5x liquidation preference plus 8% cumulative compounding dividends with participation, assuming an exit exactly 2 years after XYZ Fund's investment:

Equity Holder	% Ownership	Preference	Remainder	Total
Founder 1	17.575%		$1,127,830	$1,127,830
Founder 2	17.575%		$1,127,830	$1,127,830
ESOP	21.85%		$1,402,167	$1,402,167
Angel	3.00%	$249,960	$192,517	$442,477
XYZ Fund	40.00%	$3,332,800	$2,566,896	$5,899,696
TOTAL:	100%	$3,582,760	$6,417,240	$10,000,000

A word of advice to any would-be investors enthralled by the scenario above: while the outcome is undoubtedly great for investors, keep in mind that successful exits after a single round of investment is the exception rather than the rule. Should the company need further funding, subsequent investors will look to existing arrangements and ask for the same treatment. The hurdle rate for positive return for the existing investors will not look nearly as rosy if there were another $70 or $80 million of subsequent investments piled on top, each with 1.5x preference (and likely ahead of the earlier investors' preference), which means an exit will have to clear $120 million before the earlier investors (with their now junior preference) see a dime of return.

As the old adage goes, winning cures all ills, and if a company were to sell itself for $1 billion after having only raised $2 million or even $20 million, then all the liquidation preference, multiples and cumulative dividends will not amount to much more than noise.

Conversion

As we have touched upon previously, while the founding team (and the ESOP) hold ordinary shares in the company, investors hold *preferred shares* in the company with a myriad of preferential rights over the ordinary shares. One salient feature of preferred shares is that they are convertible into ordinary shares of the company at any time at the election of their holders.[61] This is also the mechanism that permits the investor in the example above to receive its proportionate share of the sale proceeds instead of being stuck with receiving its original investment amount (i.e., getting none of the upside).[62]

---

61 Typically, the conversion ratio is 1-to-1, subject to the adjustments we will discuss below.

62 In contrast, for *participating* preferred shares, such shares would

Mandatory conversion

Although preferred shares are convertible at any time at the election of their holders, there are certain events in which the preferred shares should all convert into ordinary shares and thereby terminating the preferred shares' preferential rights. One such event is IPO of the company, as public investors will have little tolerance for pre-existing shares bearing superior rights such as dividends and liquidation preferences. As a matter of practice, essentially all companies that go public will go public with only ordinary shares and no preferred shares outstanding. And so that is one scenario where the company (as well as most of the shareholders) has an interest for the conversion to be automatically triggered to prevent individual preferred shareholders from holding up the IPO process by refusing to convert their preferred shares into ordinary shares and forestall the company from going public.

In addition to the above, there would typically be an additional prong of automatic conversion triggered by the election of a majority (or some higher threshold) of the preferred shares. This is done more for utility reasons, giving the company and its preferred shareholders a path to potential recapitalization, restructuring and reorganization without needing to get unanimous approval from all preferred shareholders. But this prong would typically only come into play in a downside scenario where some preferred shareholders are not willing to give up their preferences and privileges.[63]

---

participate in the distribution of the remaining proceeds without having to convert into ordinary shares, but calculation of the amount receivable out of the remaining proceeds is done on an as-if converted to ordinary shares basis in any event, so we are not suggesting the convertibility is necessary for participating preferred shares.

63 One such scenario is referred to as "pay-to-play" where existing investors who fail to continue to support the company by investing their proportionate share in subsequent financings lose some or all their preferences and privileges in their preferred shares.

Anti-dilution protection

Anti-dilution protection is a concept that is intrinsically tied to conversion. In a nutshell, anti-dilution protection means that, to the extent the company issues additional securities at a price below the price paid by the existing investors, existing investors would be "made whole" through the anti-dilution protection.[64] There are 2 types of anti-dilution protection, *weighted-average* and *full ratchet*, which are best illustrated with examples.

Example:

> To recap, ABC Company had raised $2 million from XYZ Fund at $3 million pre-money valuation, $5 million post-investment valuation, resulting in XYZ Fund holding 40% of ABC Company following the investment on a fully-diluted basis.
>
> Now suppose ABC Company needs to raise an additional $1 million from a new investor at a flat valuation (i.e., $5 million), following the investment, the new investor would own 16.67% of ABC Company ($1 million ÷ ($5 million + $1 million) = 16.67%), and XYZ Fund would own 33.33% of ABC Company ($2 million ÷ ($5 million + $1 million) = 33.33%). XYZ Fund has been diluted, but not *overly* diluted, because the round was done at a flat valuation.
>
> Now suppose if instead of the round being done at a flat valuation, ABC Company instead raised an additional $1 million from a new investor at a $3 million pre-money valuation (ouch!). Following the investment, the new investor would own 25% of ABC Company ($1 million ÷ ($3 million + $1 million) = 25%), and XYZ Fund would own 30% of ABC Company (($3 million x 40%)* / ($3 million + $1 million). XYZ Fund has been *overly* diluted to the tune of 3.33% and must be made whole, and the mechanism
>
> * This is the new pre-money valuation multiplied by XYZ Fund's ownership percentage of ABC Company.

---

64 The name *anti-dilution* is a bit of a misnomer since any time the company issues securities, dilution occurs. So what *anti-dilution protection* protects against are excessive dilutions due to the company issuing additional shares at a price lower than the price paid by the investors.

for adjusting XYZ Fund's series seed preferred shares' conversion ratio to achieve that goal is called *weighted average adjustment*.[**] It takes into account both the magnitude of the reduction in valuation as well as the amount of new securities issued. As one might infer from the example above, the larger the new financing is, the more *overly* diluted XYZ Fund will be, and the larger the weighted average adjustment will be.

In contrast, under the same scenario, a *full ratchet* adjustment would mean that XYZ Fund would have its investment repriced to the new valuation, which (hold on to your seats) means ABC Company's valuation is now $1 million (since the $3 million pre-money valuation given by the new investor includes the $2 million originally invested by XYZ Fund, which is being repriced, so we need to back out that $2 million from the $3 million pre-money valuation, which leaves just $1 million...). After the financing, the new investor will still own 25% of ABC Company, but instead of 33.33% of ABC Company, XYZ Fund will own 50% of ABC Company ($2 million ÷ ($1 million + $3 million[***]).[****] Unlike weighted average adjustment, full ratchet adjustment is only price-dependent; the magnitude of adjustment is based purely on the reduction in valuation and is completely independent from the amount of new securities issued.

[**]   So instead of 1-to-1 conversion ratio, after the adjustment, each series seed preferred share will be convertible into 1.111... ordinary shares. For simplicity sake, this example illustrates an adjustment based on fully-diluted ownership of XYZ Fund (i.e., 40%), whereas the prevalent adjustment calculation in the market would be based on outstanding securities (including options and warrants, but excluding unissued ESOP reserve), which is referred to as *broad based weighted average anti-dilution protection*. Still other formulations are possible, such as only counting outstanding voting securities or even only counting outstanding preferred shares. As the denominator for the adjustment becomes smaller and smaller, the magnitude of the adjustment becomes bigger and bigger. There are various rationales for using one basis for adjustment over another (that we will not get into for this book), but the takeaway is that broad-based weighted average adjustment is the prevalent mechanism in the market.

[***] $1 million adjusted pre-money valuation + $2 million from XYZ Fund + $ 1 million from new investor.

[****] Once again, the actual implementation would be through conversion ratio adjustment, where XYZ Fund's series seed preferred shares will be convertible into 1.666... ordinary shares.

The adjustment of conversion ratio represents an elegant solution to the problem of anti-dilution protection because a company's ownership percentage and (as we will see below) voting power among shareholders are all calculated on an as-if converted to ordinary shares basis. Since distribution, share ownership after the IPO, and voting are all calculated on an as-if converted to ordinary shares basis as well, an adjustment of conversion ratio automatically confers upon investors an adjusted ownership percentage following dilutive issuances without the need by the company to issue additional shares – everything is written into the company's constitutional document and self-executing.[65] Note that because only the conversion ratio is adjusted, the actual number of outstanding series seed preferred shares *does not* change, and neither does the per share or the aggregate liquidation preference amount of the series seed preferred shares.

There are various rationales given for using weighted average adjustment versus full ratchet adjustment. Weighted average adjustment is the norm because it puts investors back to the same ownership percentage it would have had if subsequent issuances were done at a flat valuation. In contrast, ratchet adjustment is designed to preserve the *value* of investors' investment (notice how XYZ Fund gets "credit" for the entire $2 million investment under the full ratchet calculation above) and is usually used when there is a wide chasm between what the entrepreneurs think the valuation of the company is and what the investors think the valuation of the company ought to be (assuming that such chasm doesn't simply result in the investment not happening altogether).

---

65 In contrast, in China, which does not permit multiple classes of stock or conversion, conversion price adjustment is not a mechanism available for anti-dilution protection, so the parties will have to agree in advance on the mechanism for anti-dilution protection (which is typically done through make-whole transfers for nil consideration among shareholders).

There are a variety of scenarios and situations where the company (as well as investors) will have a legitimate interest in issuing shares at a lower price than the price paid by investors. For example, option issuances pursuant to ESOP at the price paid by investors will probably not be all that attractive to recruits and potential hires, so that is one common situation where shares issued at a lower price would be carved out from triggering anti-dilution protection. Other scenarios include venture debt financings, strategic collaborations, acquisitions and a variety of other customary scenarios, all of which are subject to negotiation as early as the term sheet stage.

Other adjustments

Other scenarios where adjustments to the conversion ratio occur include share split, combination or other recapitalizations. Instead of having to issue additional series seed preferred shares or ordinary shares to investors, the company can achieve the same outcome simply by adjusting the conversion ratio of the preferred shares.

Example:

ABC Company thinks the price of its ordinary shares is too high, which is making recruiting and hiring difficult because the price of its options is too high. As a result, ABC Company undertakes a forward share split where every ordinary share is split into 2 shares. Instead of issuing additional series seed preferred shares or ordinary shares to its investors, the conversion ratio of ABC Company's series seed preferred shares is simply adjusted from a 1-to-1 conversion ratio into a 1-to-2 conversion ratio.

Redemption

After wading through the relatively dense subjects of liquidation preference and conversion, we now come to the comparatively straightforward subject of redemption, which in a nutshell gives investors the ability to demand repurchase of their shares for a pre-determined amount, subject to certain conditions.

Redemption amount

Investments in startups are investments made with hopes of big multiples in return on investment. That means if a redemption is triggered, it signals a failure scenario, because no amount of redemption premium can hope to compare to what the company may achieve in the event of an IPO or a successful sale of the company (such as WhatsApp and Instagram to Facebook).

In that sense, redemption provision is a downside protection similar to liquidation preference as well as one of the mechanisms that guards against the founders getting too comfortable running the company as a cash cow without thinking about a path to liquidity for the investors. From that perspective, a 1x return (or return of capital) plus accrued interest as shown in our sample term sheet is philosophically consistent with the rationale for the provision.[66]

Triggers

Unsurprisingly, the redemption clause is subject to several customary triggers and conditions. First and foremost, all parties should share a common interest in allotting sufficient runway for the company to achieve what it had set out to accomplish, and from that perspective, a redemption trigger that's exercisable, for example, 6

---

66 Note that this is another place where cumulative dividends can crop up and result in additional payments to investors.

months to 1 year after the investment obviously would not make a whole lot of sense. In terms of time horizon, redemption triggers are typically set at three to seven years following the initial investment.

There are certain other scenarios which investors will want to have the right to trigger redemption prior to the agreed-upon date. Another frequently seen trigger provides that investors may trigger redemption if the company breaches its representations and warranties. A redemption in this case is viewed as an additional remedy for investors to claw back their investments from the company in the event of a breach by the company.

Payment schedule

From the company's point of view, it is worth considering structuring redemption as installment payments (e.g., over a two or three-year time span in equal installments instead of in one lump sum) because payment of the redemption price is not a trivial sum, especially for the kind of company that is subject to a redemption election from its investors (i.e., a company going sideways). That is why installment payments spread over time is potentially important for preserving the company as a going concern.

Voting

As we briefly touched upon previously, preferred shares of a company typically vote together with ordinary shares as a single class on an as-if converted to ordinary shares basis. The corporate law of most jurisdictions favored by venture investors provide that different classes (such as ordinary shares vs. preferred shares) and series (such as series seed preferred shares versus series A preferred shares) only vote separately if the rights of such class or series is adversely affected in a manner different from the other classes and series.

Protective provisions

Because the preferred shares vote together with the ordinary shares, a conundrum for investors is how do they protect the rights, preferences and privileges they have bargained for while being a minority shareholder in the company[67]? In light of that, market practice is that investors would be entitled to a set of *protective provisions* where fundamental changes to either their securities or to the company itself will require approval by investors before such acts may be undertaken by the company. Customary items or events covered by protective provisions include:

- selling the company;
- selling all or substantially all assets of the company;
- restructuring the company;
- issuing new securities with rights, preferences or privileges greater than or equal to investors' securities;
- changing any of the rights, preferences or privileges attached to investors' securities;
- changing the number of authorized shares of the company;[68]
- declaring dividends, making distributions or repurchasing outstanding shares;[69]
- changing the size of the board;

---

67 Notwithstanding our example where the preferred investors end up with a majority of ABC Company's voting power.

68 Changing the number of authorized shares means potentially more shares available for issuance, which can potentially impact investors' ownership percentage in the company (notwithstanding investors having anti-dilution protection and preemptive rights).

69 These are all viewed as potential end runs around the liquidation preference waterfall and/or leakage of capital from the company.

- incurring material amounts of debt;[70] and
- agreeing to do any of the foregoing.[71]

Of course, other events and circumstances falling under the protective provisions may be negotiated between the company and investors.

Investors give a lot of thought to scenarios in which they need to protect their investment in the company. From the company's perspective, the consideration is generally more about (1) protecting its ability to make quick decisions, (2) maintaining its flexibility in daily operations and (3) freedom to pursue future fundraisings and strategic opportunities.[72]

Board seats

Despite protective provisions that guard against fundamental changes being made without investors' consent, ultimately the management authority of the company is vested in its board of directors. Therefore, from institutional investors' perspective, it is imperative that they have an appointee to the company's board of directors, because directors (1) have unfettered access to the company's books and records (unlike shareholders) and (2) are active participants in the company's decision-making process with respect to major undertakings not delegated to officers.[73]

---

70 Debt is senior in priority in repayment vis-à-vis shares, so in a sense debt can be viewed as a company security with super preference.

71 This clause prevents (or at least undermines the validity of) contracts entered into by the company committing to do any of the prohibited acts.

72 Some of the decision-making authority for operationally-related events may be offloaded to the board of directors.

73 In contrast, shareholders typically do not have (and should not want to have) any right to be involved in managing the company. In most jurisdictions, the legal theory of limited liability of

Due to key decisions being made at the board level, investors for the most part will want to have a designee on the company's board of directors. Structuring the board of directors then becomes a critical item in any investment.

From the company's perspective, investors should not have an overwhelming number of designees on the board of directors, which would give them the power to dictate the direction of the company. On the other hand, investors typically want to ensure that their designees have a significant voice at the table instead of being mere participants with no meaningful impact on the outcome of decisions. Hence, for typical venture investments, the structure of the board is set up with an odd number of directors with equal representation from management (i.e., initially the founding team) and the investors, with the final seat being occupied by a "neutral" individual. For example, a board of directors with three seats typically will have one director designated by the founders, one director designated by the investors and with the third director being a joint designee who fits certain pre-agreed criteria.

The devil is truly in the details when it comes to board seat designation rights. Special attention should be paid to various conditions and voting thresholds attached to a designating party's power to designate a director. For example, would it make sense for founders to continue to be able to designate directors when he or she no longer works at the company (or worse yet, works for a competitor)? Would it make sense for an investor to continue to have designation rights if they sell 90% of their shares? What are the ramifications of an independent director being designated by ordinary shares and preferred shares voting together versus

---

shareholders rests on shareholders not being able to participate in managing the company. In other words, because shareholders have no decision-making authority, they should not be held personally liable for decisions made by the board and management.

designation with the unanimous approval of the directors? These are just some of the questions that arise (or should be asked) and get heavily negotiated in the process of firming up board composition.

The decisions may not have quite the same level of complexity versus the cascading decision tree and feedback loop of valuation/ ESOP size/anti-dilution adjustment/liquidation preference, but decisions made on board structure and composition will have a far more profound impact on the day-to-day operations as well as major operating and strategic decisions of the company.

Drag-along

Another conundrum of investors owning a minority stake in the company is in a potential exit scenario (i.e., sale of the company) where there may be disagreement between management of the company and investors on whether the potential exit opportunity is one that should be pursued. This could be due to different stakeholders' differing economic outcome in such exit and/or their different views on the company's prospects.[74] Or this could simply be due to different stakeholders' emotional attachment (or the lack thereof) to the enterprise.

To protect investors in such scenario, a lot of investors will ask for a so-called drag along provision at the time of investment, which boils down to a pre-defined group of stakeholders being able to force a sale of the company that meets a pre-negotiated set of conditions. The voting groups and voting thresholds required to trigger a drag-along may consist of some combination of (1) the board of directors, (2) the ordinary shareholders and (3) the preferred shareholders.

In a nutshell, the greater the number of groups and the higher

---

74 MySpace is a well-known example of this.

the voting threshold required to trigger drag-along, the more such drag-along provision will be viewed as forcibly implementing consensus and minimizing the ability of dissenters to cause trouble for potential exits.[75] Conversely, the lesser the number of groups and the lower the voting threshold required to trigger drag-along, the more such drag-along provision will be viewed as simply letting a small number of shareholders dictate the outcome for approving potential exits.[76]

---

75 This is especially true if the voting groups and thresholds are at or above what is legally required under the applicable merger statute to sell the company. In those situations, the minority cannot stop a deal from happening even in the absence of the contractual drag-along rights, so the utility of the drag-along rights in those cases is to take away the non-consenting shareholders' ability to launch a dissenters' proceeding in the courts and contest the fairness of the deal.

76 Recall that investors in most cases already have a protective provision giving them veto power over a sale of the company, a drag-along that can be triggered by investors alone will give investors full power to decide whether to accept or reject a potential exit.

Chapter 10
Shareholders Agreement

The shareholders agreement (or its equivalent) covers the remaining contractual terms set out in the term sheet. These contractual rights typically include:

- the right for investors to cause the company to register their securities;
- the right for investors to request and receive information on the company;
- preemptive rights by investors to subscribe their proportional portion of any new issuances by the company; and
- right of first refusal and co-sale against sale of shares by certain other shareholders of the company.

We explore each topic in turn below.

Registration rights

Registration is a concept that is fairly unique to U.S. securities laws. Unlike many other jurisdictions, under U.S. securities laws, when a company "goes public," it means one or both of the following:

- The company has *registered* a specific lot of securities for offer and sale to the public; and/or
- The company has voluntarily or involuntarily become a company subject to public reporting requirements.

A registration of shares automatically subjects the company to public reporting requirements, while a company may become subject to public reporting requirement without ever registering any securities for offer and sale to the public. Either way, what "going public" does *not* mean in the United States is that all the outstanding shares of the company are now publicly tradeable.

For shares that have not been *registered*, the public sale of such shares continues to be subject to restrictions. While exemptions are available for the resale of unregistered shares of reporting companies, investors may not be in the position to sell their shares pursuant to an exemption for a variety of reasons. Consequently, investors need registration rights by which they can require the company to register their shares for resale.

Demand right

A *demand registration* is a request for registration that may be triggered by investors. Some demand registration rights are formulated as a right that may be triggered 6 months following the company's IPO, while other demand registration rights are formulated as a right that may be triggered at any time following the Nth anniversary of investors' investment into the company. The former formulation is purely aimed at giving investors the ability to have their shares registered for resale, while the latter formulation serves the dual purpose of registering investors' shares for resale as well as being a forcing function for the company to go for an IPO (because such investors' demand for registration could be the company's first registration of its shares for offer and sale to the public, notwithstanding that the shares being registered are investors' shares and not new issues from the company).[77] As demand registrations are herculean undertakings, typically there is a limit on the number of demand registrations a company is obligated to undertake (usually one to three).

S-3/F-3 right

While demand registrations are herculean undertakings, fortunately a so-called short-form registration becomes available to the company after a company has gone public and met certain requirements.[78] Because these registrations are far less overbearing, there is usually no cap on the absolute number of these registrations a company is obligated to undertake (but there is typically a cap on the frequency of these registrations a company is required to perform (market norm is no more than two in any 12-month period)).

---

77 Like how the drag-along addresses the scenario where management and investors do not see eye-to-eye on selling the company, a demand registration that may be triggered some number of years after the investment addresses the scenario where management and investors do not see eye-to-eye on taking the company public.

78 Short form registration statements are on Form S-3 (https://www.sec.gov/about/forms/forms-3.pdf) or Form F-3 (https://www.sec.gov/about/forms/formf-3.pdf), hence the name for this registration right.

"Piggyback" right

Unlike demand right and F-3 right, which are rights to initiate registration by investors, a *piggyback registration*, as the name suggests, is investors' right to tag along a registration initiated by the company or others and have their shares included in such registration. Typically, the company's IPO would be excluded from investors' piggyback registration right so the proceeds from the IPO can all go to the company. Practically speaking, the only term pertaining to piggyback registration right that is negotiated with any regulatory is how much investor shares may be excluded (or *"cutback"*) from registration in the event the market does not have the appetite to purchase all the shares being offered.

Lock-Up

Lastly, for the lack of a better place to put this, investors typically sign up to a lock-up provision just like all other shareholders of the company.

Information rights

Information rights confer upon investors the right to receive annual, quarterly and sometimes monthly financial statements of the company, as well as a business plan for each coming fiscal year. Usually investors will require the financial statements to be prepared in accordance with an agreed-upon accounting standard (e.g., U.S. GAAP or IFRS), with the annual financial statement being audited by a reputable accounting firm. The information rights section would also set forth deadlines for the company to deliver the materials to investors. In addition to recurring information obligations, investors are typically also entitled to inspect the books, records and facilities of the company and discuss the company's affairs with management. Because the right to access company information is an expansive one, investors also typically agree to confidentiality provisions to hold all information in confidence and only use them for the limited purpose of monitoring their investments in the company.

Preemptive rights

Preemptive rights, as the term suggests, means that when the company issues new securities, existing investors would have the right, to the exclusion of all others, to purchase a certain portion of the newly issued securities of the company. Philosophically, the concept is intended to protect investors against dilution. As we previously discussed, anti-dilution protection only protects investors from excess dilution caused by a decrease in valuation. However, even in an up round, investors' percentage ownership in the company will decrease. To solve that problem, investors interested in maintaining their ownership percentage in the company ask for the contractual right to purchase their proportional share of any securities of the company issued in the future.

Example:

To recap, ABC Company had raised $2 million from XYZ Fund at $3 million pre-money valuation, $5 million post-investment valuation, resulting in XYZ Fund holding 40% of ABC Company following the investment on a fully-diluted basis.

Now suppose ABC Company needs to raise an additional $1 million from a new investor at a flat valuation (i.e., $5 million). Following the investment, the new investor would own 16.67% of ABC Company ($1 million ÷ ($5 million + $1 million) = 16.67%), and XYZ Fund would own 33.33% of ABC Company ($2 million ÷ ($5 million + $1 million) = 33.33%). XYZ Fund has been diluted (but not *overly* diluted), even though the round was done at a flat valuation.

However, XYZ Fund wants to maintain their 40% ownership in ABC Company, and pursuant to the preemptive right provision, they would be entitled to purchase 40% of the new securities (leaving only 60% of the new securities for the new investor to purchase). If XYZ Fund exercises its preemptive right, it can purchase up to $400,000 of the new issuance and maintain its 40% ownership (($2 million initial investment + $400,000 preemptive right exercise) ÷ ($5 million + $1 million) = 40%) of ABC Company.*

> * Just like in our discussion of the anti-dilution protection, for simplicity sake, this example illustrates an adjustment based on the fully-diluted ownership of XYZ Fund (i.e., 40%), whereas most adjustment formula would be based on outstanding securities (including options and warrants but excluding unissued ESOP reserve).

As one might expect, issuances excluded from anti-dilution protection are also typically excluded from pre-emptive rights for the same rationale as their exclusion from anti-dilution protection. This makes sense because conceptually, while investors have an interest in maintaining their percentage ownership in the company, there are simply certain categories of issuances that need to be exempt because they address legitimate business interests, typically with the rationale that such activities ultimately will grow the value of the company and benefit all shareholders (including investors). For that reason, under both anti-dilution protection as well as preemptive rights provisions, you will almost invariably see mirror image exclusions that do not trigger these protections.

Right of first refusal and co-sale

We covered the company's right of first refusal previously and the rationale for the provision. When investors invest, they typically receive a right of first refusal as well, normally second in line behind the company's right of first refusal. The rationale for the company having a right of first refusal applies here as well, except now with the financial resources of the investors as additional ammunition to thwart unwanted transfers.

The investors' right of first refusal also represents an avenue for investors to increase their percentage ownership of the company. As such, the chilling effect it has on potential third party buyers is arguably more pronounced than the company's right of first refusal. And this is by design, because more so than keeping shares "in the family" or increasing percentage ownership, investors' goal here is to deter third parties from approaching founders and offering them liquidity to begin with, because such offers would distract the founders from their core mission of growing the company to the benefit of all shareholders.

The right of first refusal also has the perhaps unintended effect of forcing bidders to overpay for shares (in order to discourage existing investors from exercising their right of first refusal). However, to the extent a bidder does offer to overpay for shares, investors also have a co-sale right to sell their shares and correspondingly reduce the number of shares that a founder is able to sell.

Example:

ABC Company has done extraordinarily well, and an interested party offers you $1,000,000 to buy 100,000 shares. Here is the amount each shareholder may sell, assuming holders of series seed preferred shares are all entitled to co-sale right:

Equity Holder	Shares	Relative %	Amount to Sell	Shares to Sell
Founder 1	1,000,000	29.014%	$290,140	29,014
Founder 2	1,000,000			
ESOP	1,243,243			
Angel	170,697	4.953%	$49,530	4,953
XYZ Fund	2,275,960	66.034%	$660,340	66,034
TOTAL:	5,689,900	100%	$1,000,000	100,000

After running through the math, you feel a bit of a déjà vu (from the last time you thought about declaring a dividend)* and realize that because of co-sale rights, most of the benefit from getting a great price for your shares will instead be reaped by others, which makes you far less interested in pursuing the transaction.

* See Chapter 9.

Taken together, the rights of first refusal and co-sale discourage third parties as well as founders from even initiating a discussion and ensure that instead of thinking about their individual liquidity, founders are focused on growing the company and achieving a successful exit for all shareholders.

Like anti-dilution protection and preemptive rights, there are customary exclusions to rights of first refusal and co-sale.

But in this instance, since the rationale underlying rights of first refusal and co-sale is vastly different from anti-dilution protection and preemptive rights, so too are the customary exclusions, which are intended to address legitimate personal events of the founders. Estate planning and intra-family transfers are standard exclusions from rights of first refusal and co-sale and do not need an explanation. Other less frequently encountered exclusions include pledging the shares for bona fide loans and charitable contributions. In some instances, founders may successfully negotiate a blank check exclusion that permits a small amount of securities (e.g., 5% of the founder's holdings) to be transferred without triggering rights of first refusal and co-sale, which gives founders some liquidity opportunity.

Chapter 11
How To Find the Right Lawyer

When running a startup company, founders will inevitably encounter numerous complex business and legal issues. Getting professional help when needed is the best way to avoid major disasters down the road. While a good lawyer is an extremely valuable asset in navigating you through the jungle of intricate issues, a bad one can be a huge liability. Here are some insider tips to help you find the right lawyer.

Specialization

As Adam Smith pointed out in his book "Wealth of Nations", one of the central drivers of economic progress is the "division of labor". The legal industry is not an exception. What people generally refer to as "lawyers" are actually divorce lawyers, finance lawyers, intellectual property lawyers, immigration lawyer, litigators, real estate lawyer, etc..

Each category of lawyers is further divided into many sub-categories. For example, finance lawyers have the subcategory of VC/startup lawyers, banking lawyer, M&A lawyers, IPO lawyers, fund formation lawyers, etc.. You get the idea.

The "best" lawyer is always the lawyer that specializes in the exact area of practice you need help with. Take VC/startup law as an example. An award-winning full-service firm with the greatest number of lawyers around the world may not have a specialized VC/startup practice. In this case, lawyers practicing in related areas of law cover VC/startup cases as and when they come along. Not only are they unfamiliar with the up-to-date market practice and the relevant issues (and incur more time cost doing research as a result), priority tends to be given to other work that is the firm's main practice focus.

It is quite easy to find out the main practice focus of any lawyer in today's internet age. Any proper law firm's website will have a dedicated page for each partner of the firm, stating in detail that partner's practice area with a list of his or hers most recent transactions done. Pick the one who specializes in the exact area you need help with and has done the greatest number of similar transactions.

Finding a lawyer

Like finding many other good things in life, a recommendation is the most effective way to find a suitable lawyer. If someone you strongly trusts recommends a lawyer who did a similar transaction, chances are he or she can't be too far off target. Just remember to always go back to the lawyer's webpage to make sure his or her practice area matches your needs.

In the absence of a recommendation, an internet search is also a good way to find a decent lawyer. The key is to be as specific as possible to narrow down your search. For example, search for "Singapore tech startup lawyer" instead of "good lawyer". You will find forums and websites relating to the type of lawyers you searched for and from there, shortlist a few whose practice area matches exactly what you need with a long deal list similar to your project at hand.

Filtering process

Once you have a few lawyers with potential, the next step is to make initial contact via email. Make sure your email covers the following areas clearly and concisely:

- who you are;
- the background of the case;
- which kind of help you need; and
- when you need it.

You can also request for an initial meeting to explain in person and to assess the lawyer's professional capability and suitability. Usually such an initial meeting is free of charge.

If there is no response to your email after 3 or 4 days, you can drop this lawyer off your list. This either means he or she is not very interested in your business or is not good enough to handle a case. Choose the ones that respond quickly to initiate a meeting.

During the first meeting, asking questions regarding general market practice in the area you need help with is a good way to assess how up-to-date the lawyer is in his or her specialization. You can also ask specific questions to judge if the lawyer:

- has good professional knowledge;
- has good communication skills;
- is a problem solver; and
- is commercially savvy.

Remember that after telling you what you cannot do, a good lawyer will always propose a practical alternative that achieves a similar result. The not-so-good ones just tell you what cannot be done and wait for you to come up with an alternative (and the bad ones can't understand what you are asking).

To summarize, a good lawyer usually ticks the following boxes:

- specializes in the exact area of law you need help with;
- has done many similar transactions recently;
- is service oriented and responds quickly;
- is commercially savvy and a problem solver; and
- communicates well, can explain complicated issues clearly.

Finally, it's helpful to know that lawyers charge by the hour so your ability to consolidate key issues and communicate in a clear and concise manner will help you save significant time cost.

May you find the best to help when in need!

About Jerry Ku

Jerry has spent his entire legal career as business lawyer and advisor to emerging growth companies throughout their lifecycles. Jerry represents a wide variety of technology companies in artificial intelligence, clean tech, fintech, media, software and telecommunications industries, and serves as regular outside counsel for a number of leading venture capital firms in their investments in education, life sciences and TMT startups, which is how Jerry first met Xu.

Jerry is broadly experienced with corporate formation, structuring and governance matters, cross-border deals and structuring, venture capital financing transactions, public offerings, SEC regulatory compliance and a variety of M&A transaction structures and take private transactions involving companies based in the United States and Asia. Jerry resided in Beijing from 2013 to 2018 and focused on China-based emerging growth companies and U.S. dollar investors making invests in Chinese technology startups. During his time in Beijing, Jerry was a frequent lecturer at Renmin University School of Law.

Jerry has native fluency in spoken and written Mandarin. Jerry holds a J.D. from Columbia Law School and received his B.S., double majoring in Biology and Philosophy, from Duke University. Following his tour of duty in Beijing, Jerry now resides with his family in the San Francisco Bay Area.

About Han Xu

Xu is a specialist in venture capital, startup and finance law, who represents venture capital funds, financial institutions and startup companies all over Asia. She also regularly advises on finance, corporate and commercial matters. She is known to be highly practical, efficient and commercially oriented. Xu is a qualified solicitor in England and Wales and an advocate and solicitor in Singapore. She has many years of working experience as a senior lawyer in top U.S. and U.K. law firms.

Being a true cosmopolitan, Xu has lived in China, Japan, the United States, the United Kingdom and Singapore since her childhood and now resides with her family in Shanghai, China. Xu can speak, read and write English, Japanese and Mandarin at native proficiency. During her spare time, she likes to travel, to write, to draw and to dream.

Made in the USA
Coppell, TX
07 March 2021